READING BOOKS

FOR PROFIT

By Rebecca Harris

Published By

Clarendon House, Inc.

Copyright © 1997 by Clarendon House, Inc.

All rights reserved. No part of this book may be reproduced or utilized in any form or by any means, electronic or mechanical, including photocopying, recording, or by any information storage and retrieval system, without permission in writing from the Publisher.

Library of Congress Card Number: TX-114-384
ISBN 1-886908-07-9
2nd Edition

Printed in the United States of America

Acknowledgments

We would like to take this opportunity to thank the many people involved in the development and publication of *Reading Books for Pay*. A special thank you to the following organizations and individuals who helped make this book possible: the reference librarians at the Santa Barbara, California public library; the Society for Children's Book Writers and Illustrators; Gaughan Public Relations; Elaine Jesmer Public Relations and Publicity; the U.S. Department of Agriculture; and the many publishers who took the time to share their stories and expertise with us.

A very special thank you to the amazing individuals who have paved the way by carving out a niche for themselves reading books for pay. These dedicated and creative people are an inspiration to everyone who follows in their footsteps!

A Note from the Publisher

We have made every effort to ensure the accuracy of the information in this book. However, we cannot be held responsible for any errors that may have inadvertently been made, or for changes in any of the information since we went to print. The book is designed to provide information about reading books for pay, and is sold with the understanding that the author and publisher are not in any way engaged in or offering accounting, marketing, legal or any other professional services. In all such matters we recommend that you seek the services of a competent professional. Please always bear in mind that our sole purpose in writing this book is to inform and help you, the reader.

Table of Contents

Foreword 1

Introduction 3

Chapter 1: Overview and Fast Start 9

Chapter 2: Marketing Yourself 15

Chapter 3: Be A Publisher's Reader 25

Chapter 4: Proofreading, A Great Way to Break In 37

Chapter 5: Copyediting, Tricks of the Trade 51

Chapter 6: Indexing 63

Chapter 7: Be a Fact Checker 75

Chapter 8: Writing Blurbs and Flap Copy 83

Chapter 9: Writing Book Reviews 95

Chapter 10: Doing Research for Authors 109

Chapter 11: Reading Movie Scripts and Plays for Profit 123

Chapter 12: The Audiobook Market 137

Chapter 13: Get Your Own Writing Published! 151

Chapter 14: For Book Authors Only: Finding An Agent 167

Chapter 15: Writing Children's Books 183

Chapter 16: Writing for Magazines 193

Chapter 17: Homestead Publishing Program 205

Chapter 18: How to Read Critically 219

Chapter 19: Self-Confidence is the Key 235

Appendix A: Writer's Conferences 243

Appendix B: Writer's Organizations 249

Bibliography 253

Glossary 257

Index 266

Foreword

First of all, we thank you for choosing to invest in this book! We believe you'll find *Reading Books for Pay* to be one of the most complete books of its kind available—a resource that you will use again and again.

The information contained in this book is designed specifically for anyone who loves reading and wants to turn their talent into a money-making skill. Our researchers have uncovered the latest opportunities in the publishing industry—opportunities that most people don't even know about! Plus, you'll find chapters on writing and selling your own books, magazine articles, and children's literature—and with our "Homestead Publishing Program," you'll even learn how to publish what you write yourself!

This book will help you develop the dedication and motivation you need to make money by reading books. You'll find it easier to make the right decisions, based on the information provided. And while this book can change your career for the better, it is only the beginning of your exciting journey to success!

Use this book as your coach, guide, and mentor, and you'll soon be on your way to a rewarding, challenging, and fun new career reading books for pay!

The Publisher

2

Introduction

Welcome to the world of reading books for pay! By purchasing this book, you've taken the first step — you're about to create a whole new life for yourself based on doing something you love!

People who read books are a special breed. These days, with television, videos, and computer games all vying for our attention, you are to be commended for hanging onto your love of books! In fact, you're in good company — despite the explosion in other forms of media, there are more books being published right now than at any other time in the history of the planet!

That's good news for you, because the simple truth of the matter is, there are countless opportunities to make money by reading books — either on a freelance basis or as an employee in the publishing field. You don't have to worry about there being too much competition, either. There is MORE than enough work to go around. The secret is finding it. That's what this book is all about.

The Inside Scoop

The publishing industry is known for being very closed-mouthed about its hiring practices. Some of the jobs described in this book are practically unknown to the general public — yet they can generate an income of $35,000 a year or more for you! No doubt about it, you'll have a very real advantage over your competition after you read this book!

This book will show you how to approach publishers, writers, and other people who can offer you work reading books for pay. You'll get to know all about these jobs and the training required (if any). In some cases

4 Introduction

you may find it beneficial to start out as an employee at a publishing house until you learn the ropes. Soon, you'll have gained enough know-how to go out on your own as a freelancer.

Freelancers generally make more money than regular employees. You also have the option of working for more than one client, which can make your work that much more interesting and profitable! And there are so many advantages to working from home — like setting your own hours and being there for your children — that you'll wonder why you didn't become a freelancer sooner!

Never Say Never!

By now you may be saying to yourself, "But I don't know how to do this." Nonsense! First of all, you already have more going for you than you think. Since you sent for this book, you obviously have a strong interest in

books and reading. Over the years, you've probably read hundreds, if not thousands, of books! That means you've stored up a great deal of knowledge along the way about what makes a good book. This knowledge is already a natural part of you, and it's something you just can't get by going to school!

You see, publishers and writers won't care how much education you have, as long as you can do the job. Sometimes you might need additional training, but in most cases, you can either train on the job or acquire the skills you need by taking a couple of courses. You can make it easy on yourself simply by building on the skills you already have.

There are plenty of ways to break into the field of reading books for pay that don't require specialized training. There are opportunities waiting RIGHT NOW for someone like you, right in or near your own town — you don't have to go to New York or Los Angeles or any other big city to "make it"! This book will show you how!

Build on Your Interests

One theme we'll come back to over and over again in this book is, "Start with what you know." In other words, the road to success is a path that you've already laid out for yourself. Ask yourself the following questions:

- What are my hobbies and interests? _____

- What do I love to do in my spare time? _____

- (If currently employed) What do I like about the job I have now?

- (If not currently employed) What activities in my day do I like the best?

- What is my basic temperament? (Shy or outgoing? Detail-oriented or focused on the "big picture"?) _____

Keep the answers to these questions in mind as you read through this book. Match your personal profile with the requirements discussed for each job. If you're detail-oriented, for example, you may be very happy working as an indexer. If you'd rather write your own books instead of reading books by others, you may enjoy the challenge of getting your own writing published. And if you have a job now, you can supplement your income by writing magazine articles for the trade journals in your field!

No matter what your personal profile, rest assured that there is a job for you reading books for pay!

The Self-Confidence Factor

As you get ready to enter this new and exciting field, you may find your self-confidence is on shaky ground. That's perfectly understandable. After all, you've never tried anything like this before. But believe us, once you try it, you'll be amazed at how easy the whole process of reading books for pay really is!

It's really no different from learning to ride a bike when you were a kid. At first, it seemed impossible to balance yourself on the bike. You probably wobbled back and forth and fell off more than a few times. But how long did that last — an hour or two? And ever since, you've been riding a bike like nobody's business, right?

You'll find the same process applies to reading books for pay. When you write your first letters to publishers, you will probably feel awkward and not quite sure of yourself. But by using the examples in this book to guide you, you'll soon feel very confident when you approach publishers, writers, or anyone else in this business. And soon you'll be commanding a handsome salary for the work you do — what could be better than that?

How Much Can You Make?

There are so many money-making opportunities in this book that you need a chart to keep track of them all. That's what we've done right here, so you can see at a glance the income potential of each opportunity. Then turn to the appropriate chapter, and learn how you can get started reading books for pay!

No matter what specific job you're interested in, you'll probably find it useful to read Chapter 2, "Marketing Yourself." This chapter will give you the extra edge you need to make a good impression and get the job you want. You'll also want to give yourself an added boost by reading Chapter 19, "Self-Confidence is the Key."

Income Chart

The annual income figures below are based on a 30-hour work week for 48 weeks a year, which is typical for a freelance worker. Granted, these estimates are conservative. If you work more hours, you can expect to earn even more! Keep in mind that some of the opportunities that offer less pay are still a great way to break in, and also a great source of part-time income to supplement your regular job while you make the transition to reading books for pay.

	HOURLY RATE	ANNUAL INCOME
Proofreading	$10–$25 an hour	$14,400–$36,000
Copyediting	$12–$40 an hour	$17,280–$57,600
Indexing	$15–$40 an hour	$21,600–$57,600
Publisher's Reader	$9–$12 an hour	$12,960–$17,280
Fact Checker	$12–$25 an hour	$17,280–$36,000
Writing Blurbs and Flap Copy*	$100–$600 per book	$9,600–$57,600
Book Reviewer*	$35–$200 per book	$3,360–$19,200
Researcher for Writers	$10–$30 an hour	$14,400–$43,200
Reader for Play and Movie Scripts**	$40–$80 per script	$3,840–$7680
Reader for Audio Books***	$20–$85 an hour	$19,200–$40,800
Writing Books for Adults or Children	Advances range from $4,000–$50,000. Royalties range from 10% of cover price on hardcovers to 6–8% on paperbacks.	
Writing for Magazines	5 cents to $2.50 per word; or roughly $30–$3,000 per article	
Self-Publishing Your Own Writing	The sky's the limit!	

* Based on 2 books/week ** Based on 2 scripts/week *** Based on 10 hours/week

Chapter 1
Overview and Fast Start

This chapter is especially designed to give you an overview of the contents of this book—and by doing so, to get you started reading books for pay that much sooner!

As you'll soon learn, reading books for pay is a goal that you can achieve NOW. You don't need years of experience and training to break into this exciting field. All you need is the advice and guidance offered in this book! So use this chapter as a guide to what's inside. When you come across a topic that catches your eye, then turn to that chapter to find out more.

If you're not sure how to go about finding work, then **Chapter 2, Marketing Yourself,** is the perfect place to begin. This chapter describes what to expect when you go out looking for work in the publishing industry, the benefits of starting small, and the importance of getting yourself out and about in the publishing world. You'll learn how to get started locally and how to write letters to publishers that get results! You'll also find information here about brushing up on the basics of the English language, and on classes that can help you do just that!

Chapter 3, Be A Publisher's Reader, takes you behind the scenes at publishing houses across the country. This chapter explores the world of publisher's readers—those individuals whose sole job is to read book manuscripts! You'll be in the know about what readers look for in a manuscript, the process of critiquing manuscripts, and the role of a subject matter expert. This chapter provides you with two sample letters that will help you find work in this field, plus a sample Reader's Report which you can use to practice your newfound skills.

Now that you're out of the starting gate, check out **Chapter 4, Proofreading: A Great Way to Break In.** Proofreading is one of the easiest ways to start out reading books for pay. This chapter discusses the "eagle eye" the proofreaders are known for and how to develop this trait in yourself. You'll learn the two types of proofreading, the importance of consistency, how to follow "house style," and all about proofreader's marks. Then you'll discover how to find work, how to approach publishers, and how to get training. Last, but not least, this chapter wraps up with the good news of how much you can expect to be paid for your efforts!

Moving on to **Chapter 5, Copyediting: Tricks of the Trade,** you'll see that copyediting is a natural outgrowth of proofreading, the topic of our last chapter—and the financial rewards are even greater! This chapter explores what makes a good copyeditor, the two types of editing, and the truth about writers and writing. You'll learn the twelve top mistakes committed by writers and how copyeditors correct them. Then this chapter gives you a strategy for approaching publishers, plus suggestions for going freelance and working with authors on your own. You'll also find useful tips on training opportunities in this very interesting field.

Chapter 6, Indexing, presents one of the best kept secrets of the publishing world—and one which can have substantial financial rewards for you! This chapter covers the basics of indexing and where to learn the trade. You'll also learn how computers are used in the indexing process, from specialized indexing programs like Macrex and Cindex to a writer's forum for indexers on America OnLine. Then you'll find a discussion of indexing styles, how to break into this hot field, and how to grow your business—plus the benefits of belonging to the American Society of Indexers!

Chapter 7, Be A Fact Checker, reveals the secrets of another little-known aspect of the publishing industry. Individuals known as fact checkers are key players at magazines and publishing houses everywhere, and you can find work either on an in-house or freelance basis! This chapter starts at square one with a discussion of "what is a fact"—a more complicated issue than it might seem at first glance! Then you'll discover the methods fact checkers use to ply their trade, how to get hired, and opportunities for advancement.

Have you ever wondered who writes the "blurbs" on the back cover of a book, or the copy on the front and back flaps? Well, it could be you! **Chapter 8, Writing Blurbs and Flap Copy,** gives you all the basics on these essential jobs. You'll find detailed instructions about how to write blurbs and flap copy, plus samples of each. You'll also learn about a related field, writing new book releases, which you can break into as well.

Chapter 9, Writing Book Reviews, covers everything you need to know about one of the easiest ways to read books for pay. Chances are that you can find publications that need book reviews <u>right now</u>, in your own town or very close by. You'll learn the importance of assessing a book fairly, how to break into print, and the basics of writing reviews for newsletters, newspapers, and magazines. This is truly a great way to get paid for reading books—plus, you get a free copy of every book you review!

If you think you'd like doing research, you'll want to turn straight to **Chapter 10, Doing Research for Authors.** This chapter tells the amazing story of a researcher who made millions of dollars for his contribution to *The Book of Virtues*. Then you'll discover the nuts and bolts of doing research: how to use libraries to the best advantage, the importance of getting to know the librarians, and how to use computers for research. The world of digital information, from the Internet to CD-ROM discs, is discussed in detail. You'll also learn the secrets of doing research by phone and how to conduct successful interviews. This chapter concludes with a list of questions to ask before you begin a research project, and how to find work in this endlessly fascinating field.

Do you like movies and plays just as much, if not more than books? Then **Chapter 11, Reading Movie Scripts and Plays for Profit,** is just for you! Yes, you can be one of the lucky readers who gets paid—and very handsomely, we might add!—for providing critiques of plays and movie scripts, or screenplays. In the industry, these critiques are known as "coverage." You'll learn about the pot of gold (the Reader's Union), how to break in, and how to evaluate manuscripts. This chapter concludes with an example of coverage written by a professional in the field.

For something completely different, check out **Chapter 12, The Audiobook Market.** Did you ever wonder who the voices are behind the

12 Chapter 1: Overview and Fast Start

audiobooks you see everywhere these days? This chapter will show you how to find a niche as a reader for audiobooks! There is no shortage of opportunities to break into this rapidly growing field. This chapter describes what it takes to make it, how to practice your reading skills, finding work, and helpful publications about the field. There's even a list of audiobook publishers to get you started!

Have you read so many books that you've finally written one of your own? If so, **Chapter 13, Get Your Own Writing Published,** will be of special interest to you! This chapter guides you through the process of submitting a manuscript to a publisher. You'll learn special techniques to make your manuscript stand out in the crowd. You'll also learn the six essential ingredients of good writing. This chapter concludes with ways to market your writing and a few words of advice about professional writer's organizations.

Perhaps you've wondered about getting professional help to sell your manuscript to a publisher. If so, **Chapter 14, For Book Authors Only: Finding An Agent,** will help demystify the process and get an agent on your team! The chapter explains the role of an agent, how to find an agent, and how to write a query letter to an agent. You'll also learn the pitfalls of agents who charge reading fees for evaluating your manuscript. This chapter concludes with a list of agents and the kinds of books they're looking for.

Chapter 15, Writing Children's Books, provides you with an introduction to this very popular field—where the potential for success is truly unlimited! There's an organization that can provide you with virtually everything you need to know to get started, the Society of Children's Book Writers and Illustrators. This chapter tells you how to join this organization and explains how the SCBWI supports new writers. Among other things, every year this organization has a conference where new writers can get critiques of their work from established authors! This chapter also includes tips from a professional children's writer on a correspondence school and other writer's conferences, plus advice on getting to know the market, finding the publishers you like, and approaching a publisher.

Do you love magazines? If so, you will be very interested in **Chapter 16, Writing for Magazines.** This chapter explains the huge market that is just waiting for your article ideas! You'll find success secrets here in abundance—from the basics of requesting writer's guidelines from a magazine, to a strategy for deciding what to write about. You'll find a sample query letter too, plus a list of query letter do's and don'ts. This chapter will help you set your goals, sit down to write, build a niche for yourself in the publishing world—and last but not least, get paid! This chapter concludes with a reminder about trade journals—one of the best paying and least known markets in the magazine world!

If you've written a book, why not publish it yourself? **Chapter 17, The Homestead Publishing Program,** will show you how to do just that! This chapter explains how you can use the resources you have on hand RIGHT NOW to become a publisher yourself—at a cost so low, you'll wonder why you didn't think about doing it before! Plus, when you do the publishing yourself, you get to keep ALL the profits! From small booklets to full-size volumes, this chapter will show you how to get your book into print and sell what you've written for a tidy profit!

Chapter 18, How to Read Critically, shows you how to take your natural aptitude for reading and develop strong skills for evaluating manuscripts. This chapter has sections that apply to both fiction and nonfiction material. You'll discover the criteria used to judge good writing, the basics of story structure and how to apply them, and how to practice what you've learned. This chapter will give you a strong foundation in critical reading skills—skills that you'll use every day while you're reading books for pay.

Does all this information seem a bit overwhelming? You might need to take a look at **Chapter 19, Self Confidence is the Key.** This chapter will boost your spirits and make you want to get right out there and start reading books for pay today!

Appendix A, Writer's Conferences and Workshops, provides you with a wealth of resources for furthering your knowledge of reading and writing. And **Appendix B, Writer's Organizations,** is bursting with networking opportunities for you!

Finally, we provide a **Glossary** to acquaint you with specialized terms in the publishing industry, as well as a **Bibliography** for further reading. With all these resources at your command, we think you'll be well on your way to success in reading books for pay before you know it! So use this book as your guide, and remember that you too can make it happen. Great success to you!

Chapter 2: Marketing Yourself

You've heard it said a thousand times: "put your best foot forward." This chapter is about how to do just that — how to get your foot in the door reading books for pay! You are your own best asset, and we'll be talking about how you can best present yourself to the publishers who are your prospective employers.

Of course, you've also heard it said that "a journey of a thousand miles begins with a single step." Rest assured, this chapter is the first step on your road to financial rewards from reading!

Review the material in this chapter carefully. Some of the topics covered here will also be referred to in other chapters; but you'll be ahead of the game if you start right now. We'll cover how long it takes to break in, how to get started, getting out and about, writing query letters, and brushing up on basic skills.

Marketing yourself is an everyday affair that pays big dividends over time. When you know how to market yourself, your confidence will show. You'll make a favorable impression on the people you meet. Even if they don't have work for you right away, they'll remember you when the next opening comes around. That's the goal of marketing yourself successfully: to be the person who stands out in the crowd. So follow the advice in this chapter, and you'll be heads above the rest!

Breaking In

The good news is that there's more work in the publishing industry than you can shake a stick at. In fact, it's quite easy to find work right away.

But finding enough work to support yourself on a full-time basis can take some time.

How much time? That depends on you and on the specific profession you choose. It might be a matter of months, or a year or two. The great thing about so much of the work we describe in this book is that you decide how much or how little you want to work. Once you've made a few contacts and word-of-mouth takes over, you'll have all the business you can handle!

I know this is true from direct experience. In the seven years that I've run my own freelance writing and publishing business, I've never once advertised. Well, actually, I take that back. Once I ran a $35 business card ad in a program brochure sponsored by a local Women's Day Conference. Did it bring in any new business? No. But by growing my business steadily by word-of-mouth, I'm now making over $50,000 a year! How did I do it?

Stay Safe and Start Small

There's no substitute for staying safe and starting small. When I first went out on my own, I quit my job completely and wasn't sure what I was going to do next. Sure, a few people I knew around town promised me work — but it never materialized. I did get lucky, and several clients came my way during my first few months in business — so I made enough to pay my expenses, barely!

Then one day, I got a phone call about a job I had applied for at the local university. It had been so long since I applied for this job that I'd forgotten about it completely. The upshot is, I went for an interview the next day and got the job. It was part-time — just 20 hours a week — as an editor for a campus magazine. And because this job was classified a professional position, it had full health benefits!

I didn't know it then, but that job was just what I needed. I kept it for the next year and a half while I built up my freelance business. Then, I was able to go out on my own once and for all, and I've never looked back!

The moral of the story is: don't go cold turkey at the beginning. Hold onto your job until you've really built your business to the point where it can support you and your family. You'll be glad you did!

Get Out And About

I live in a small city that supports a thriving publishing community. I learned early on that the way to get work is to see and be seen. There is a downtown area about six blocks square where most of the publishing business in town is located. In the early days of my business, whenever I was short of work, I used to take a walk downtown over my lunch hour or during the afternoon. Without fail, I would run into someone I knew who would say, "I was just thinking about you! There's this job I need some help with...."

Now, you may or may not live in a town or city where simply stretching your legs will get you work. But I hope the point is well taken. You must keep yourself visible among the people you wish to work for. There are many avenues you can choose — here are a few of them:

- Attend public events that involve writers and readers, like book signings, lectures, book fairs, and publication parties.

- Join book clubs and writer's groups.

- Take classes to improve your writing skills and reading skills.

- Attend writer's conferences and workshops.

I suggest that you sit down and make a list of the resources available to readers and writers in or nearby your community. If you're not sure, ask your local bookstore, community college, or adult education program if they have a list of events and organizations for people who love books, both writers and readers. Then, choose the events that appeal to you and show up! Developing contacts and friendships through avenues like these is just about the best strategy I know to find work reading books for pay!

Get Started Locally

When you're first getting started, look for some small jobs that you can do for organizations in your own community. While these jobs may not pay much, you can use them as a stepping stone to get better paying work later. Every job you do, no matter how small, is something that you can note on your resume. So when you're first starting out you might want to volunteer your services. For example, if you belong to a club, whether it's the Rotary Club or Rose Society, you might volunteer to write articles for their newsletter.

Maybe you can proofread or edit the local Chamber of Commerce magazine. Maybe you can write book reviews for your local weekly newspaper — or offer your services as a fact checker. If you're interested in being a reader for audio books, practice by volunteering as a reader to the blind. If you know someone who's written a book, volunteer to help them with publicity or arranging a book signing at your local bookstore. And if you're a writer yourself, you might self-publish one of your stories and sell copies of it around town!

You get the idea. Whatever niche in the publishing world appeals to you, be creative and think of a way to start doing that very thing RIGHT NOW in your own community. The wonderful people and opportunities in my town never cease to amaze me. I guarantee that you'll find the same thing is true in your town, too, no matter where you live!

Branch Out With Letter Writing

While you're getting out and about, you should also spend some time in the comfort of your own home pounding out letters to publishers on your typewriter or home computer. Throughout this book, you'll find sample letters that you can use as a basis to write your own. The purpose of these letters is to ask the specific publishers you are interested in if they have any work for you.

You see, while the personal contacts you make by getting out and about can't be beat, you can't possibly meet all the people who need your services that way. Spend some time finding out who the publishers are in your area and what their needs are. There are several lists of publishers in Volume II to help you get started. You can increase your odds by consulting the lists of hundreds upon hundreds of publishers in *Writer's Market* and the *Literary Market Place*, the two bibles of the publishing industry. *Writer's Market* is available either at your local library or bookstore; *Literary Market Place* is a massive volume that you'll find at your library reference desk.

Here's what to do: when you review the lists of publishers, first identify those that are located close enough to where you live so that you could go in for a personal appointment. Then, pick the ones you think you might actually like to work for. If you're not interested in widgets and know nothing about them, there's no point in writing a letter to *Widget World Magazine*!

Letter Writing Tips

In my small city, I have obtained work from many publishers I didn't know by writing query letters. I always make my letters brief and to-the-point — never more than a page long. Usually I enclose my latest resume or a sample of some writing I've done. Also, I always enclose my business card. This combination usually gets me a phone call and an interview — and at the very least, if there's no work available at the moment, the publishers will save my information on file.

When you're just starting out and have few, if any, credits to your name, simply send a letter without a resume. This chapter includes a sample letter to give you the idea. Adapt it for your own use, and you'll be pleased with the results! Then, as you build more and more work experience, you can work it up into a resume later.

Today's Date

Arnie Editor
Anytown Chamber of Commerce Magazine
111 Main St.
Anytown, USA 09090

Dear Arnie Editor:

I am writing to inquire whether you need editing or proofreading assistance with the Anytown Chamber of Commerce Magazine.

As a long-time resident of Anytown, I have read the Chamber of Commerce Magazine for years. Because I am so familiar with the publication, I think that I would be able to offer you especially good service.

I have an AA degree in English from Anytown Community College, and I am currently taking the "Principles of Editing" class offered in adult education.

Please contact me at the address and phone listed below. Thank you for your time, and I look forward to hearing from you.

Sincerely,

(signature)

Amy Jones
435 Park St.
Anytown, USA 09090
444-5555

P.S.—Don't Forget the Yellow Pages!

Sometimes it pays to let your fingers do the walking! Your local Yellow Pages is an excellent source of contacts for query letters. I review the Yellow Pages every year when the new phone book comes out. You never know what publishers might be doing business right around the corner!

And P.P.S. — I've learned over time that it's always better to send a letter than to call an unknown publisher out of the blue. Every publisher I've ever known would prefer to have a neat, typewritten letter in front of them and be able to call you back at their convenience. So, although it may be tempting to pick up the phone, I strongly urge you to resist that temptation — in the long run, the rewards will be far greater if you send a letter instead!

The exception, of course, is if you DO know the person already — or if you know their best friend, or if you live in a very small town where just about everyone knows just about everyone else. In that case, a phone call might be just the ticket!

Brush Up on the Basics

There are a few basic skills that you need to have in your marketing tool kit. The good news is, even if you're a little rusty, it won't take any time at all to get back up to speed!

First and foremost, you need good spelling, grammar, and writing skills to read books for pay. Exactly how good? Well, for spelling, you can get a lot of help from your computer's spellchecker — but even that wonder of the modern world won't catch every error. Some computers have grammar checkers too, but they're even less foolproof than the spellcheckers.

So don't rely on your computer to bail you out! Instead, set a little time aside and educate yourself. There are a few inexpensive books that can really help you out in this regard. Try *The Elements of Grammar* by Margaret Shertzer (Collier-Macmillan Publishing Company), which includes a chapter on spelling. This book, and many others like it, are readily available at your local library or bookstore.

One of the most famous guides to writing well is *The Elements of Style*, by William Strunk, Jr. and E. B. White (Macmillan Publishing Company). This tiny book first appeared in 1959 and it is a classic in its field. Chances are, whenever you're not sure how to put something in writing, this book will be able to help you out. I recommend it highly for your home bookshelf!

Classes in English Usage

Don't be shy about taking a course in basic English usage through your local community college or adult education program. These courses are usually free or available at a minimal cost. If there are no classes like this in your area, there is a great correspondence program offered by the United States Department of Agriculture. In fact, this correspondence program is so good that we'll be referring to it many more times throughout this book!

The USDA offers a whole series of courses under the heading, "Enhancing Language Abilities." These courses consist of anywhere from 7 to 12 lessons which you do at your own pace, in the comfort of your own home. Some of the course titles include:

- Clarifying Words that Confuse

- Expansion of Vocabulary Knowledge

- Writing Sentences and Paragraphs Effectively

- Better Letters

For more information and a free catalog about these courses, call the USDA at 202/720-7123 or write:

Correspondence Program
Ag Box 9911
Room 1114, South Agriculture Building
14th St. and Independence Ave. S.W.
Washington, D.C. 20250

Think Like a Pro!

My last word of advice is: if you want to be treated like a professional, you must think like one and act like one! Here's a story to illustrate my point. Once, during my first meeting with a new client, he looked me straight in the eye and asked me, "Are you a professional?" Even though I'd been working as a freelancer for about three years at that time, I gulped. But I managed to say "Yes." By the way, that man became one of my best clients, and I'm still working for him today!

Even if you're at the very beginning of your career reading books for pay, think of yourself as a professional. Don't forget that after you read this book, you'll know far more than just about anyone else who wants to enter this field. Think and act like a professional, and you'll be treated like one! It's that simple!

Which brings us to our final point....

Don't Mention This Book

When you go out into the world looking for work reading books for pay, don't tell them you read this book! Why not? Well, like I just said, the whole point is to present yourself as a professional. Let the editors and publishers you talk to think you got so smart from many sources, not just a single book. For example, if you say, "I want to be an editor because I read a book called Reading Books for Pay," you're not going to impress anyone. On the other hand, if you show you've got an understanding of what it takes to be an editor, they'll be more than happy to give you a try.

What they don't know won't hurt them — but it will certainly help you! So use the wealth of information contained in this book to break through all barriers to success. Focus on the knowledge this book gives you and put that knowledge to good use — and you'll be one of the so-called "lucky ones" to get your foot in the door!

Chapter 3:
Be a Publisher's Reader

If you really love reading books, and love to share your opinions about them, you'll be amazed to learn that you can get paid for doing that very thing! It's called being a publisher's reader, and this chapter will explain what it's all about.

The role of the publisher's reader could be described as playing God — or at least, God's assistant. It's up to a publisher's reader to determine the fate of unsolicited manuscripts that come in "over the transom." The reader must answer the question: Is this manuscript publishable or not? Readers can be either freelancers or full-time staff people. They report to the editorial or trade departments at large publishing houses all across the country.

The Two Types of Book Manuscripts

Most publishing houses deal with two types of manuscripts: solicited manuscripts and unsolicited manuscripts. Solicited manuscripts are those that come from agents or that are commissioned, such as new books from authors who have already written best sellers. Solicited manuscripts rarely go to a publisher's reader; instead they are assigned to editors or editorial assistants.

On the other hand, unsolicited manuscripts are those that arrive in the mail and gather in huge heaps, known in the publishing industry as the "slush pile." Publishers hire readers to go through these manuscripts and decide whether any of them are publishable or not.

Some publishers have an official policy of not accepting unsolicited manuscripts — though this policy may or may not be actually true. Other publishing houses are so small that the owners read all the manuscripts themselves. Many small presses are specialized by subject and handle just a few new titles a year anyway.

If you get to know a small publisher personally, you might be able to talk your way into reading manuscripts for them, especially if you have expertise in the subject area. However, the best opportunities for publisher's readers are definitely at the larger publishing houses.

Diamonds in the Rough

If a manuscript is unsolicited, there's a very slim chance it will be selected for publication by any publishing house, large or small. Since everyone knows this is true, why do publishers hire readers at all? The answer is, because there is always the chance of finding a diamond in the rough. Publishers know there's a chance that their next blockbuster is buried in the slush pile, and the reader's job is to find it and bring it into the light of day.

People in the publishing industry like to tell the story of *Zen and the Art of Motorcycle Maintenance* by Robert M. Pirsig, a best seller in the 1970s which was first circulated among readers at a publishing house. The readers all loved it and fought strongly for the book's publication. The result was a tremendous success for the book when it reached the public — even today, it remains a cult classic!

The excitement in being a publisher's reader lies in the possibility that you, too, will discover an incredible manuscript in the slush pile. Sure, you can expect to read plenty of clunkers along the way — but you'll be developing an eagle eye for what works and doesn't work in a manuscript. And that skill is worth good money to you, both now and in the future!

What Readers Look for in a Manuscript

- First and foremost, is the manuscript a "fit" with the publisher? Does the publisher generally publish other books on the same topic? A publisher that specializes in romance novels will not waste any time checking out a cookbook. It may seem obvious, but authors make this mistake more often than you might think!

- Next, the reader must address marketing issues. Is this a financially viable book for the publisher? A manuscript may be brilliant, but it will never get published unless the publisher can sell copies of this particular book — and lots of them — successfully in the marketplace. Every publisher has its own criteria for judging marketability, and they will provide you with these criteria once you begin working as a publisher's reader.

- If the manuscript gets past subject matter and marketplace issues, the next important step is to evaluate it for quality and the personal qualifications of the author. Is the book well-written? Does it move the reader? Will people like it? Is the author a leading expert in the field, or just someone off the streets with an opinion? For example, if a book is written on a medical subject, the author had better be a doctor or another highly educated individual. If it's by Joe Schmoe, chances are it will be rejected immediately. (Publishing can be a heartless industry!)

The Critique

Most manuscripts that are seen by readers make the rounds of more than one reader — sometimes as many as four. Usually it takes only one reader to "kill" a manuscript. On the other hand, a popular manuscript goes on from reader to reader accumulating those all-important "recommends."

Some publishing houses have standard forms for their readers to fill out and record their evaluations. These forms range from the very simple to the extremely complex. At some publishing houses, readers are required only to give the old yes (recommend) or no (pass).

A reader's report typically includes a brief summary of the book's contents, followed by the reader's evaluation of the book. For fiction books, the evaluation provides a critique of content and structure, including a discussion of plot, characterization, dialogue, and ideas. For nonfiction books, the criteria are basically the same: the book must earn passing grades in subject matter and marketability, plus general readability, content, and structure. A reader should not be surprised when asked to back up a critique with specific page references.

Subject Matter Experts

The description above basically applies to fiction books — novels, short stories, and the like. When it comes to nonfiction, you may find opportunities to be a publisher's reader for pay if you can present yourself as a subject matter expert.

The saying "Just the facts, ma'am," definitely applies to the job of a subject matter expert. What you'll be doing is verifying if the facts in a manuscript are correct — and more. Since you're the expert, you'll know if the writer left out important information about the field; you might even have firsthand knowledge about new developments that would affect the writer's conclusions!

If you're like most people, there's an area that you know more about than the rest of the general population — whether it's baking a cake, auto repair, crafts, or a million other topics. For example, say that you've been doing macrame for 20 years and have never found an adequate book on the subject. What you can do is approach the publishers of craft books and tell them about your area of expertise. The next time they have a book come in about macrame, they can send it on to you for an expert critique!

Of course, if you're really good at what you do and truly know more about the subject than anyone else, you might want to consider writing a book yourself! See Chapter 13, "Get Your Own Writing Published!" and Chapter 17, "Homestead Publishing Program," for ideas.

Meanwhile, here's a sample letter that you can use to introduce yourself to a publisher as a subject matter expert.

Getting Yourself Hired

While a degree in English or in the liberal arts may help qualify you as a reader, you often don't even need that much to get in the door. If you're well read in a specific subject area, or have gained knowledge through real life experience, that may be enough to give you the edge you need. Don't fake it, though — your background must be genuine! A high school diploma plus evening courses in English through adult education is also a good combination.

It will be easy for you to convince a publisher to hire you as a freelancer or staff person if you really love books. After you get started, you might even find that you want to make a career out of reading books for pay! Many big-time editors and publishers got their start as readers. (This is the "mail room" of the publishing industry!)

The publishing field is truly an insider's market, through and through. You might approach these magic gates by seeking an internship. As an intern, you may work for free or for very low pay at first — but once the publisher gets to know you, you can easily shift over into a "real" job or regular freelance work.

Today's Date

Josephine Editor
Anytown Publishing House
123 Main St.
Anytown, USA 45678

Dear Josephine Editor:

I have always admired the books on crafts published by your company, and I wonder if I might be of service to you as a subject matter expert.

My area of expertise is macrame. I have developed macrame as an art form over the past 20 years and have taught many classes on creating unique objects with unusual materials.

I am enclosing a copy of a newspaper article that appeared in the *Anytown Gazette* about me last year. As you can see, around here they call me the "Macrame Lady"!

Please contact me at the address and phone below if I can be of service to you.

Sincerely,

(signature)

Elizabeth Expert
8910 Central Ave.
Anytown, USA 45678
123-4565

If you have friends who know people at publishing houses, get them to introduce you. Ask how you can groom yourself to get hired by a particular publisher. Keep in touch with your contacts and ask to be told if people are leaving the company.

There is a partial list of United States publishing houses, large and small, in Volume II. Send a query letter to every publisher in your immediate area. Pick the ones that are close enough so that you can go in for a personal appointment if necessary. Don't forget that you can find many more publishers to contact in resource books like *Writer's Market* or *Literary Market Place*, both of which you can find at your local library or bookstore.

Be sure to include a resume or summary of your experience, and explain that you're interested in being a publisher's reader. It's better to write than to call — publishers tend to be very busy and may be abrupt with you on the phone. You certainly don't want to offend these people before you even meet them!

Here's a sample query letter that you can use to send to publishers. By all means, try to address this letter to a specific person. You can get the names of specific individuals at a publishing house from a directory like *Literary Market Place*; or, better yet, call the publisher yourself and ask for the name of the person who hires readers.

See and Be Seen

The bottom line is that there's no replacement for personal contacts to break into the publishing business. Improve your chances by expanding your options. Take classes, attend writer's conferences, go to booksignings at your local bookstore — in other words, wherever there's a chance of meeting authors and publishers, go there! See and be seen. Introduce yourself and ask intelligent questions. Show up over and over again. It won't take long before people realize you're serious about reading books for pay and they offer you a chance to prove yourself.

Today's Date

Joe Editor
Anytown Publishing House
123 Main St.
Anytown, USA 45678

Dear Joe Editor:

I'm aware that you sometimes hire freelance readers. I would appreciate it very much if you would place my letter and resume on file for this purpose.

As you will note from my resume, I am attending night classes at Anytown Community College, where I serve on the editorial staff of the college literary magazine. My main interests in reading are recent fiction and how-to books, two areas that I know your firm specializes in.

I would be available to work on either a freelance or part-time basis. Would it be possible for me to write a report on a sample manuscript so that you can evaluate my skills? If so, please contact me at the address and phone below.

Sincerely,

(signature)

Rebecca Reader
567 Park St.
Anytown, USA 45678
456-1323

An Insider's Note

When you first start out as a publisher's reader, the pay varies from $25 to $50 for a single critique. And once you get your foot in the door, you have the potential to move on to a staff position at a publishing house, with the lure of an upwardly mobile job in the future.

If you are intelligent, love books, and have an eye and ability to critique in a precise manner, you can be an invaluable resource to a publishing house. The opportunity to work at home as a freelancer is another plus. And you'll be part of an industry that most people can only dream about — with the chance to be the first person to read a best seller before it's even published! What could be better than that for a true lover of books?

Sample Reader's Report

If you'd like to try your hand at writing a reader's report, pick out any book from your bookshelf and use this sample form. Write several to get the hang of it. Then you'll be that much more confident when approaching publishers — you'll know you can do the work!

Sample Reader's Report

Date: _____

Reader's Name: _____

Book Title: _____

Author: _____

Summary of Contents: _____

_____

_____

_____

_____

_____

Reader's Comments: _____

_____

_____

_____

_____

Recommend or Pass? _____

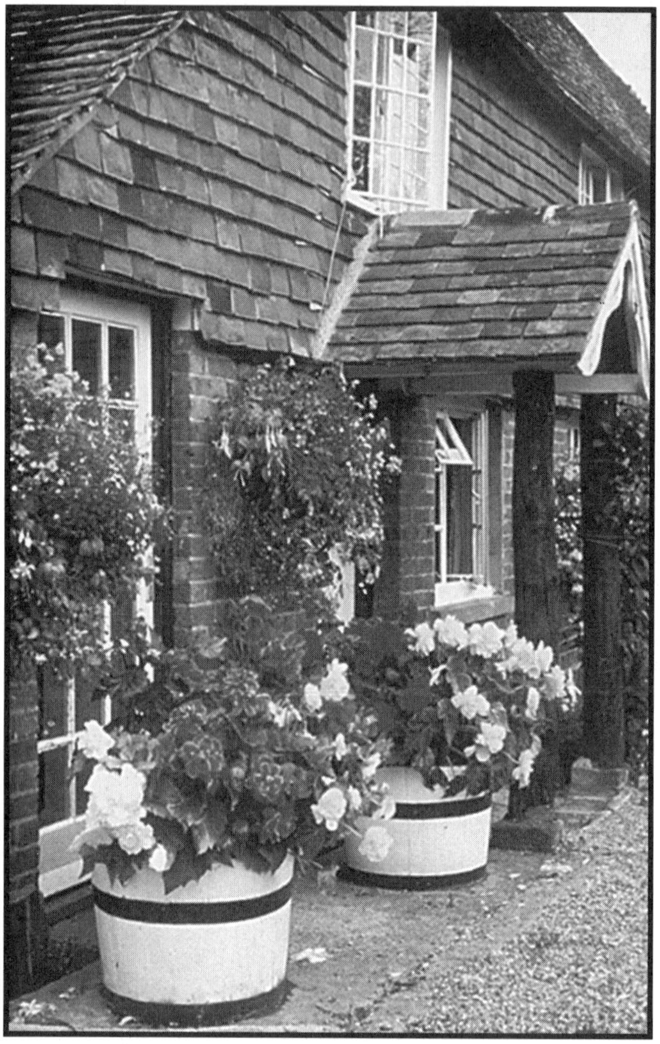

Chapter 4
Proofreading:
A Great Way to Break In

Are you the kind of person who always notices misspelled words in the newspaper, or whatever it is you happen to be reading? (And do your friends get tired of you pointing them out?) You just might have the eye for detail necessary to be a proofreader. If so, count yourself lucky. Proofreading is one of the easiest and fastest ways to make money reading books!

You don't need any special kind of education to be a good proofreader. You just need the knack of being able to spot errors that other people pass right over. Proofreading is work that you can start right now, today, and the only equipment you need is a red or blue pencil and a dictionary! Now, there are very few jobs in the world that ask so little, yet give so much in return!

When I started out reading books for pay, my very first jobs were proofreading jobs. I did proofreading for people who published newsletters, people who published articles, and yes, people who published books. By completing each job on time and to the best of my ability, my reputation grew. Soon I had all the proofreading work I could handle—and the same thing could happen to you!

Editors and writers are ALWAYS on the lookout for good proofreaders. Some publications have proofreaders on staff, but a great many use reliable freelancers. This is one job market where you can write your own ticket! This chapter will explain what is involved in proofreading and how you can get started NOW. Proofreading represents a great opportunity to break into the world of reading books for pay, so don't let it pass you by!

The Eagle Eye

What makes a good proofreader? It's that "eagle eye," the ability to spot a mistake after 20 other people who read the same page never even saw it. You can develop this ability with practice; you probably have it to a certain degree already. Besides, after you get a few proofreading jobs under your belt, you'll be sailing through manuscripts with ease, amazing everyone with your accuracy and attention to detail!

Types of Proofreading

There are basically two types of proofreading. One is when someone hands you a finished article or book and asks you to "just check it over, please." Then you simply read the piece for spelling and grammatical errors, marking any corrections with a red or blue pencil. This basic kind of proofreading is what you do for newsletters, articles, and most other short pieces that you are given by writers or editors.

The second type of proofreading involves checking an article or book against a previous version of the same piece, or against any other kind of background material. It's a little more complicated than the first type of proofreading, and it's often used for longer articles and books that contain technical material. You must go back and forth between Version 1 and Version 2, comparing them with each other and noting any items that were left out or transferred incorrectly with a red or blue pencil. Then, of course, you must always be checking for spelling and grammar mistakes as well!

Consistency and Style

Editors and writers rely on proofreaders to ensure consistency as well as accuracy in their printed documents. Whether you're proofreading an article or a book, it's very important to make sure that the same words are used in the same way throughout.

For example, the names of states can either be spelled out or abbreviated—California, or CA. Whatever style is used must be adhered to faithfully from beginning to end. Oftentimes, it's not a matter of one or the other being right or wrong—it's just that a decision must be made which one to use, and then the proofreader must make sure that the decision is followed.

House Style Vs. No Style

If you proofread for publishers, they will often provide you with a "house style" sheet. This sheet lists the word usages that the publisher prefers. All you have to do is follow the sheet. Depending on how particular the publisher is, the style sheet may be anywhere from one page to 20 pages long! Most are a few pages in length. They are really not at all intimidating, but rather give you virtually all the instructions you need to do your job well.

If there is no house style sheet to fall back on, the professional approach is to make up your own style sheet as you go along! Every time you must make a decision to establish consistency in a document, make a note of your decision on a separate piece of paper. By the time you've finished proofreading, you have a record of all the decisions you've made, and you can review them easily with the editor or writer you're working for.

Proofreader's Marks

Proofreading has a universal language all its own: the language of proofreader's marks. A chart with proofreader's marks is printed on the following pages. These symbols are understood just about everywhere in the publishing world. No matter what kind of material you proofread, any editor or writer will be able to understand these marks!

For an illustration of how these marks are used, see a guidebook like *The Chicago Manual of Style, 14th Edition,* available in your local library or bookstore. Make a photocopy of this proofreading chart and keep it with you while you do your first proofreading jobs. Rest assured, all it takes is a little practice using these marks, and they'll be like second nature to you!

A Philosophy of Proofreading

Some proofreaders like to throw their weight around, making sure that every rule of grammar is followed to the letter. They love to fill a page up with proofreader's marks. It gives them a sense of power, something to live for.

Personally, I am NOT one of those people! Sure, I passed through a phase like that, but I got over it. Over the years, I've learned it's more important to be flexible than to be a self-proclaimed policeman (or policewoman).

Don't get me wrong—it's absolutely essential that you make the manuscript you're proofreading the very best that it can be. But my point is this: if the entire manuscript uses the abbreviation CA instead of California, and there's no preference marked on the style sheet you've been given, and if you just happen to have a personal preference for seeing the word California spelled out—get over it, and leave all those CAs in!

Here's a one-sentence summary of my philosophy of proofreading: <u>Change something ONLY if you KNOW you are right.</u> If you're not sure, or if you feel yourself getting self-righteous, put on the brakes! Life is short, and your job as a proofreader is to make life easier for everyone, not more difficult!

The Deadline Factor

One thing you'll learn right away about proofreading is that everybody wants the job done ASAP! Proofreading is usually the last step before an article or book is sent to the printer—and even if it's the newsletter for your local coin collecting club, someone's probably tapping their foot, waiting for you to finish proofreading so they can get it over to the copy shop before the meeting at 7 pm tonight!

Sample Proofreader's Marks

✄	Delete, take out	⌒	Close up entirely; take out space
stet	Let it stand-(all matter above dots)	⌣	Less space between words
¶	Begin a paragraph	eq #	Equalize space between words
No ¶	No paragraph.	‖fl.L. flR‖	Flush left, right
run in	Run in	ls	LETTER-SPACE
flush ¶	No paragraph indention	#	Insert space (or more space)
lc	Set in LOWER CASE or LOWER CASE	⊙	Period
caps	SET IN capitals	ʾ	Comma
clc	Lower Case with Initial Caps	⊙	Semicoln
sm caps	SET IN small capitals	⊙	Colon
rom	Set in roman (or regular) type	⌄ʾ	Apostrophe or 'single quote'
ital	Set in italic (or oblique) type	⌄ʾʾ ⌄ʾʾ	Quotation marks "quotes"
lf	Set in lightface type	?	(circled in red) "query" to author
bf	Set in boldface type	!/	Exclamation point
⌐	Move to right ⌐	=/	Hyphen
⌐	Move to left	N M	Dash (show length)
ctr	]Center[	( )	Parentheses
⌣	Lower (letters or words)	[ ]	Brackets
⫽	Straighten line (horizontally)	SP	Spell out (20 qt.)
⌐⌐	Elevate (letters or words)	OK w/c	OK "with corrections"
tr	Transpose letters in a word	OK a/c	or "as corrected"
tr	Transpose enclosed in ring matter	↓ ↑	Push down, or up
lead	Insert lead between lines	see L/o	See layout
		X	Bad letter

So be prepared to work on tight schedules, under deadline pressure. Once people know that you do proofreading, it won't be unusual for you to get a phone call like this: "Hello, Mary? This is Susan from Anytown Chamber of Commerce Magazine. Our regular proofreader called in sick, and the magazine has to be at the printer by 5 pm tomorrow. Can you help us out?"

Here's my advice: if you really want to get started reading books for pay, ALWAYS say yes to phone calls like this! Rearrange the rest of your life if you must; work all night if you must; but ALWAYS say yes! You'll be amazed at how fast the word spreads—for example, Susan will tell her colleagues, family, and friends, "You know Mary who does freelance proofreading? If it hadn't been for her, we wouldn't have met our deadline this week!"

Plus, you'll discover other perks of being someone your clients can count on. I'll never forget the first time I received a dozen roses from a grateful client—believe me, it made staying up all night to get the job done worthwhile. As time goes on, you'll discover other benefits as well—from being invited to the company picnic or Christmas party to receiving a bonus for a job well done. As a reliable freelance proofreader, people will consider you part of their team, even though you're not on the payroll!

Finding Work

So, how can you go about finding work as a proofreader? The first, and best, way is to start with your very own self and the people you know. What clubs and organizations do you and your friends belong to? How many of them have newsletters and other publications that need proofreading? Make a list. My guess is that you'll have quite a list on your hands! And don't forget about where you work, too—many companies publish newsletters or monthly information sheets for their employees.

Now that you've done this very easy research, all you have to do is approach the person in charge of the publication and say, "Do you need any help proofreading the newsletter? I'd like to help out!" Nine times out of ten, the newsletter chairman will be overwhelmed and only too grateful for your help. You'll probably get a reaction like, "Really? Great! The next issue comes out in a week. Can you do the proofreading this weekend?"

When opportunity strikes, say YES! It doesn't matter if your first few jobs pay nothing, or next to nothing. What you're doing is getting practice, and building up a portfolio that you can use to get more work in the very near future. Keep sample copies of every job you do, because soon it will be time to . . .

Expand Your Contacts

Think of other places around town that publish newsletters or small magazines. Maybe your town has a "What's Doing" magazine that comes out once a week. Maybe there's an entertainment newspaper or a fitness club that sends a newsletter to its members every month. Maybe the YMCA, YWCA, or other family organizations in your town have newsletters. Make a list of all these organizations.

Then, simply place a phone call to each place on your list, and ask to speak to the person in charge of the newsletter or magazine. Say, "I do freelance proofreading, and I wonder if you could use some help with your publication." Once again, when you get a nibble, do whatever it takes to get the job and get it done on time. Now that you have some experience, you can expect to start getting paid—it may not be much, but it will be enough to get you over the next hurdle in your proofreading career . . .

Business Cards and Ads

Here's another idea. Put up a sign in your local copy shop that you do proofreading. You might even get a business card printed up that has your name, the title "Proofreader," and your phone number. Most copy shops will print up nice-looking business cards on plain white stock with black lettering for under $30. You never know who will see your card and give you a call!

When I first started working as a proofreader, I tried placing an ad in the classified section of my small-town newspaper. You'd be amazed at the response I got from that tiny ad! Not only did I get three great clients out of it, but one of them became a very close friend! Now, this ad was inexpensive to run, so the business I got from it made it very worthwhile for me. Before you take out an ad in your local paper, check the rates and be sure to get the cheapest rate possible!

Approaching Publishers

By now you've had plenty of practice in proofreading. You've saved samples of all the newsletters and small magazines you've worked on. You've even earned something for your efforts. And you've done all this in a matter of months. Congratulations! Now you're ready to approach the big leagues—the major book and magazine publishers of the world.

You'll find lists of these publishers in Volume II to get you started. There are hundreds upon hundreds of publishers listed in books like *Writer's Market,* available at your local library or bookstore; and *Literary Market Place,* available at your local library's reference desk.

Your goal is to find publishers in your area—close enough so that you can go in for an interview, and interesting enough so that you'd want to work for them in the first place. Some of the larger publishers may have staff positions available for proofreaders; many more will hire proofreaders on a freelance basis.

When approaching larger publishers where you don't know anyone on staff personally, it's far better to make your initial contact by letter rather than by phone. Get the right editor's name to use on your letter by consulting the *Writer's Market* or *Literary Market Place.* Here's a sample letter to get you started.

Today's Date

Annie Editor
ABC Books
333 Publishing Way
Any City, USA 11223

Dear Annie Editor:

I am writing to inquire whether you have a need for proofreaders. I have experience working as a proofreader for various publications in Anytown, USA, including *What's Doing in Anytown* and *The Anytown Gazette*.

My education includes an AA degree from Anytown Community College. I am available to work on either an in-house or freelance basis.

Please contact me at the address and phone listed below if any openings are available. I would welcome the opportunity to come in and meet with you at your convenience.

Thank you for your time, and I look forward to hearing from you.

Sincerely,

(signature)

Patty Proofreader
110 Grammar Way
Anytown, USA 11223
456-9877

Specialize If You Can

Do you have specialized knowledge in a the medical field, legal field, engineering, or any other business or industry? If so, you can put that knowledge to good use as a proofreader. The best part is, people with the know-how to proofread technical documents can command top dollar for their work—$25 an hour, or even more!

Don't be shy about approaching any publisher or business if you have education or work experience that sets you apart from the crowd. One area that might be of special interest to you is trade industry journals. There is a brief listing of such journals in the back of this book; you can find a more extensive list in *Writer's Market*. Believe me, once the people in your field know about you, they'll be beating a path to your door!

A Proofreader's Tool Kit

Like we said at the beginning of this chapter, the tools of the proofreader are few. Invest in a few red and blue pencils. (Blue is the traditional color of proofreaders, but I find that most of my clients these days prefer red.) Post-it notes can be good, especially when you're first starting out—if you change your mind, you just remove the post-it!

Then make sure you have a good dictionary by your side at all times. I actually have three dictionaries on hand—Webster's New Collegiate Dictionary, the American Heritage Dictionary, and the Oxford English Dictionary. (This last one is a huge single volume which you practically have to read with a microscope!) But if I could only have one of these, it would definitely be Webster's.

It would also be helpful for you to own a book on English usage. My favorite is *The Elements of Style,* which I've already described in Chapter 2. This is a small, almost pocket-sized book which you can find in just about any good-sized bookstore. It's clear and easy to understand—a true classic in its field, and well worth the very small investment to have it on your home bookshelf!

There are many other books available on English usage, so you might want to browse the shelves at your local bookstore or library to see what's available. If you'll be doing proofreading in a specialized area, such as medical or legal documents, you may need special dictionaries and reference works that are appropriate to your field. Sometimes the publisher you work for will provide you with these extra reference materials, or you can use them at the office library.

Training for Proofreaders

Occasionally, you may be able to find a course in proofreading at your local community college or adult education program. But even if you can't, you'll probably find any course in English usage to be helpful. Ask someone in the English department for advice if you're not sure which course to take.

Then there's the United States Department of Agriculture course in proofreading. This is a correspondence course with 10 lessons that you can complete at your own pace, in your own home. You simply send in the lessons as you go and they are reviewed and graded by the instructors. This course teaches you to proofread by doing actual exercises that familiarize you with proofreading symbols. For more information, call 202/720-7123 or write: Correspondence Program, Ag Box 9911, Room 1114, South Agriculture Building, 14th St. and Independence Ave. S.W., Washington, D.C. 20250.

Money in the Bank

So as you've gathered by now, the money you can make from proofreading depends on exactly what kind of material you proofread and who you do it for. When you first start out, you may choose to do a few jobs for free or for very little money—less than $10 an hour—just to get yourself going. This is a good idea. As you gain experience you can gradually increase your fees. You'll find lists of these publishers in Volume II to get you started.

There are hundreds upon hundreds of publishers listed in books

Publishers pay in-house proofreaders very little money—you'll be lucky if you can get as much as $10 an hour. So if you want to work in-house for awhile to get experience, great—but be prepared to move on to freelancing soon. The money is simply better!

Just about anywhere in the country, a very respectable fee for freelance proofreaders is $15 an hour. It goes up from there. If the material you're working on is technical or complex, you can command $25 an hour—sometimes more! And if you have a reputation for accuracy and reliability, you can charge $25 an hour even if the material isn't technical at all!

When people trust you to do the job right, they'll be willing to pay you twice as much as a less experienced person—simply because they know they can count on you! So strive to complete your proofreading jobs on time, and strive for 100% accuracy—and it won't be long before your efforts are richly rewarded!

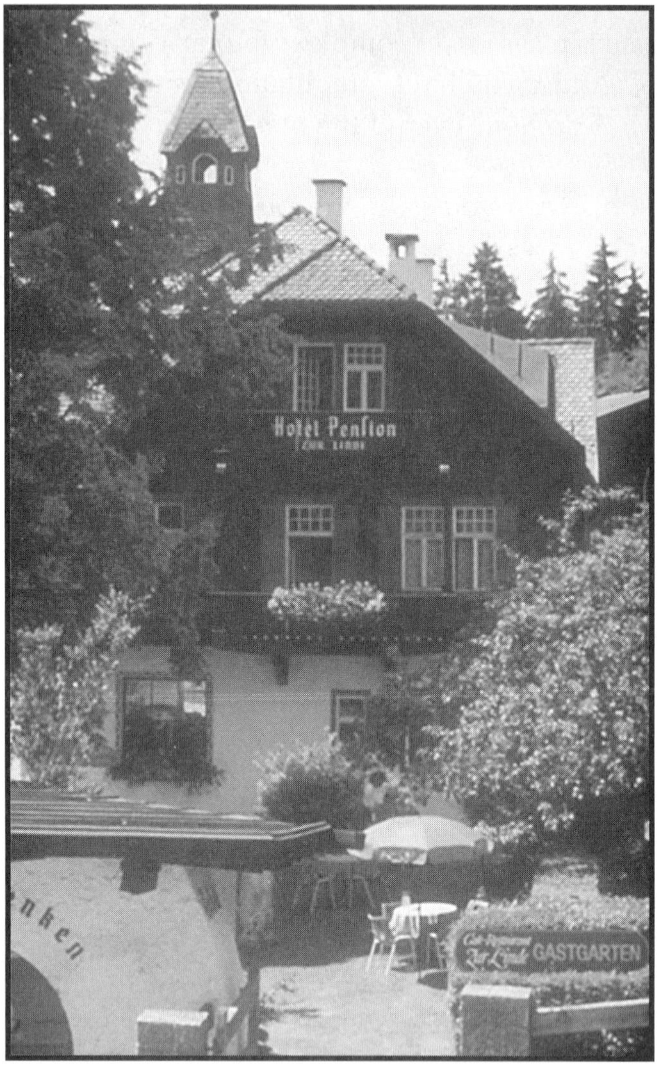
Hotel Pension
GASTGARTEN

Chapter 5
Copyediting:
Tricks of the Trade

Copyediting is a second cousin of proofreading. Chances are, if you like proofreading and find you're good at it, you'll like copyediting as well! As you proofread a manuscript, it's only natural to think to yourself, "I know how to make this sentence (or paragraph, or chapter) sound better . . . I wish I could just change a few words here and there." Well, as a copyeditor, you can!

The job of the copyeditor is to take an article or manuscript and massage it into tip-top shape—getting all the kinks out of it, so to speak. Sometimes this requires almost a sixth sense about the "rightness" of the words on the page. But if you love books, all the reading you've done over the years has by now instilled that sense in you!

The good news is, you can make even more money for copyediting than you can for proofreading. An experienced copyeditor can make up to $40 an hour! And it won't take long at all for you to get the experience you need—read on for details!

What Makes A Good Copyeditor?

Do you have the qualities to make a good copyeditor? As we already mentioned, first and foremost is the love of books—that's half the battle! As for the other traits you need, you probably have some of them already, and the rest you can learn quickly. Perhaps the most important skill is the ability to pay close attention to details—plus, the ability to keep these details fresh in your mind as you read the manuscript from start to finish. Patience and persistence are helpful. And if you need to speak to an author directly, courtesy, tact, and professionalism are an absolute must!

Good copyeditors are worth their weight in gold to publishers—so if you can prove your worth, you'll be indispensable to them!

The Two Types of Editing

Basically, editing falls into two categories. The first is a sort of glorified proofreading, sometimes called "mechanical editing," where you check a manuscript for grammar, spelling, punctuation, and consistency throughout the document. (See the section on "Consistency and Style" in Chapter 4 for the basics on this process.) Most publishers will provide you with their own style sheets to guide you.

The second kind of editing is more substantial, and is appropriately known in publishing circles as "substantive editing." What you do is dive below the surface of a manuscript to edit the actual contents and presentation. At its height, this process can involve rewriting and reorganizing an entire manuscript. With experience, you will come to enjoy and look forward to projects that involve substantive editing. Besides, this kind of editing pays more and can be more rewarding to you on a personal level. There's a great feeling that comes when you see a book in the bookstore and you know that your editing helped that book reach its full potential!

The Truth About Writers and Writing

Let me share with you something I learned during my college days when I took a class on editing. In this class we examined many books—some of them classics by famous authors—and we learned that, in many cases, different editions of the same book had different words in them. Either the author would make changes, or sometimes the publisher would make changes without the permission of the author! And this applies to works of fiction as well as nonfiction!

The point is, a book is a living, breathing thing. When you hold a book in your hand, it's easy to think of it as being cast in concrete. You assume that one day the author said, "My book is finished," and that was the end of it. But this is not always the case.

In fact, that's the very reason why new editions of books are produced—to correct any errors or omissions that appeared in previous versions. The book itself is just one point in that process. Take this book you're reading right now, for example. It will be continually revised and updated as new information becomes available. It's just part of the continuum that starts with writing, moves on to editing, and then goes on with more editing and rewriting into infinity!

So you can see that as a copyeditor, there is plenty of room for you in the publishing process. If you work for a publisher, you might find yourself involved in the same book project for a year or two—from the initial editing and rewriting to revisions that are made after the book is published. You'll get to know each book inside and out. In fact, "your" books will become like children that you hate to see grow up and leave home!

Just remember: the truth about writers and writing is, nothing is cast in concrete. Writing can always be made better, and as a copyeditor, you are the one to do it!

What Copyeditors Look For

Even experienced writers make mistakes. As a copyeditor, your job is to identify those mistakes and turn them into wonderful, readable writing. And while just about anyone can correct basic errors in a manuscript, it takes a trained eye to identify problems with the writing itself and make appropriate suggestions to improve the piece.

What follows is a list of the twelve top mistakes committed by writers. When you read a manuscript, be on the lookout for these twelve items. With a little practice, you'll be able to pinpoint these problems at the drop of a hat—and writers will be only too grateful for your intelligent and helpful suggestions!

The Top Twelve Mistakes Committed by Writers

1. Writing sentences in the passive voice.

Here's an example of the passive voice: It was raining and thundering. Here's an example of the active voice: Rain came down in sheets, and the thunder roared.

See the difference? Passive voice is boring and slow. Active voice picks you up and takes you somewhere! As an editor, watch out for excessive use of passive voice in a manuscript. Replace "was" and "were" with verbs that show action.

2. Using the same words over and over.

Most writers have a few pet words that they just love to death. They use these same words over and over, sometimes three or four times on a single page—or more! Writers will be very grateful to you for pointing out this kind of repetition, since it's something they just can't see themselves. Your job as a copyeditor is to suggest synonyms, or words that mean the same thing, to bring variety and life to the manuscript.

3. Using too much punctuation.

Some writers just can't get enough of commas, semicolons, dashes, or ellipses (. . .). Now, there's nothing wrong with any of these punctuation marks; it's just that when they're used over and over, it has the same effect as using the same word over and over. Keep your writer from being showy and self-conscious about punctuation. Consult a good basic manual on English usage, like *The Elements of Style,* for guidance in this area.

4. Using too many contractions.

Contractions—you're, I'm, isn't, aren't, they'll, etc.—signal an informal style that doesn't always suit the publisher you're working for. As you can see, contractions are used freely in the book you're reading right now—but we're definitely on the informal end of the scale! Some magazines, for example, prefer that contractions be used only in reporting conversation. When in doubt, check the publisher's style sheet or ask for advice.

5. Writing "purple prose."

Purple prose is a disease that often afflicts beginning writers. The symptoms are too many adjectives and too much description. Here's an example: "The rich, red tropical sun rose brilliantly over the sparkling azure blue water, spreading its glorious warmth over the dewy dandelions, sensuous snapdragons, and sleepy morning glories that opened their blue mouths wide to taste the delicious dawn." Ugh! Help your writers simplify their writing and avoid the pitfalls of purple prose!

6. Overusing pairs of adjectives.

Pairs of adjectives are another way writers sometimes overdo it. Here's an example: "The eerie, pale moon rose over the dreary, black mudhole." One good adjective usually works better than two. Two adjectives together usually detract from the content of the sentence—and this blunder is usually the sign of a writer lacking in self-confidence. Help the writer by trimming the fat, choosing the strongest adjective, or suggesting a new adjective if appropriate.

7. Overusing cliches.

Does the writer use a cliche at every opportunity? Too many cliches detract from the message at hand. Some famous cliches are: He made a mountain out of a molehill; She was footloose and fancy free; He talked a blue streak. You get the idea. As a copyeditor, it's part of your job to help writers express their thoughts in an original way!

8. Overusing 50-cent words.

It's a bad sign if you have to grab the dictionary and look up every other word in an author's manuscript. Too many unfamiliar words are a turnoff to most readers. What do you do if you're reading an article in which you feel the author is showing off or talking down to you? You put it down without finishing it, right? As a copyeditor, you have the power to keep this from happening to your writers. Help them keep it simple!

Of course, if the subject matter is technical, that's a totally different story. What we're talking about here is the equivalent of overusing vocabulary words in daily conversation.

9. Making all sentences the same length.

Does the writer use all short sentences, or all long sentences? Varying sentence length is one of the characteristics of good writing. The right combination of short, medium, and long sentences actually helps hold the attention of the reader and move them along from one page to the next. Make sure your writer follows this important principle!

10. Adding information that's off the subject.

Ask yourself these questions about the manuscript or article you are editing: is all the information relevant to the story at hand? Do all the people mentioned add something to the story? If not, it is your duty as copyeditor to note where the writer has strayed and get the manuscript back on course.

11. Using too many words.

Some writers simply go on and on, with no sense of how to get to the point. They pile on the adjectives and adverbs (-ly words). They make general statements that don't go anywhere. They use three or four words when one word would do. There's only one cure for a manuscript with these failings: it must be cut down to size! Eliminating unnecessary words is the forte of many a well-respected editor.

12. Being too general.

General statements suck the lifeblood out of any manuscript. Help the writer be as specific as possible. When you see the words "a lot", ask how many, exactly? When you see the word "beautiful," ask, in what way? Take a look at the books you enjoy the most. Invariably, you'll see that they are packed with details that allow you to hear, see, feel, touch, taste, and completely participate in the scene being described. That's why it's possible to get lost in a book! Whether it's fiction or nonfiction you're editing, the principle is the same: ask for details, details, details.

Working With Publishers

One of the best ways to get your feet wet as a copyeditor is to work for a publisher. That way, you'll be around plenty of people who can offer you guidance as you learn the art and craft of editing.

Though it can be very valuable to take classes in editing, the best training of all happens on the job. Here's a step-by-step plan to work your way into the field:

- Start out as a proofreader. See the strategy in Chapter 4 for breaking in as a proofreader.

- Let the people you do proofreading for know that you are interested in copyediting. Encourage them to try you out on a simple article or manuscript.

- Find a "mentor"—an experienced editor who can guide you through the ins and outs of copyediting. Seek out this person for advice on your first copyediting jobs.

- Gradually increase the amount of copyediting work you do, and decrease the amount of proofreading you do.

- As you gain experience, approach other publishers and writers to obtain work on a freelance basis.

No matter what kind of publisher you're working for—be it a newspaper, magazine, book publisher, or whatever—you will be expected to use certain reference books and follow certain stylistic preferences. These requirements will be reviewed thoroughly when you start the work.

Especially at first, your work will be judged by how well you can use these reference works and meet the publisher's standards—so vow to become familiar with the entire process and do the best job you can. Believe me, people will stand up and take notice when you do an outstanding job—and that means you'll get even more work in the future!

If you're not familiar with the publishers in your area, use the list in Volume II to get you started. Refer to *Writer's Market* (at your bookstore or library) and *Literary Market Place* (at your library reference desk) for hundreds more listings. Consult your local Yellow Pages, too. Follow the same procedure outlined in Chapter 4; contact only those publishers to whom you live close enough to go for an interview. Resist the temptation to call the publisher directly; instead, make a lasting impression by sending a letter something like the one on the next page (adapted to your own situation and circumstances, of course).

Going Freelance

After you've worked for a publisher for awhile, you'll have the experience and contacts you need to move into freelance work as a copyeditor—and you'll earn more money to boot! Probably the most you can make at a regular "salaried" copyediting job is $15 or so an hour. But as a freelancer you can earn much more—anywhere from $20 to $40 an hour!

There are several ways to build enough freelance contacts to "make it" on your own. You can branch out from the contacts you've made on the job; many freelancers find that their first client becomes the firm they used to work for! Also, let your friends, family, and community know what you're up to. Build your business by doing some volunteer copyediting for a club or nonprofit organization—it's a perfect way to get your name and experience known! See the strategy outlined in Chapter 4 for getting proofreading clients; the same strategy can be used for copyediting as well.

Working With Authors

Through contacts in your own community, you will find authors who need someone to work with them on their book manuscripts. This can be a great opportunity for you as a beginning (or experienced!) copyeditor—or, it can be a disaster. I'll give you an example of each.

Today's Date

Anthony Editor
ABC Books
333 Publishing Way
Any City, USA 11223

Dear Anthony Editor:

I am writing to inquire whether you have a need for copyeditors. I have experience working as a copyeditor for various publications in Anytown, USA, including *The Anytown Community College Sentinel* and the *Anytown Theater Review.*

My education includes an AA degree from Anytown Community College. I am currently taking night classes in English through adult education. I am available to work on either an in-house or freelance basis.

Please contact me at the address and phone listed below if any openings are available. I would welcome the opportunity to come in and meet with you at your convenience.

Thank you for your time, and I look forward to hearing from you.

Sincerely,

(signature)

Connie Copyeditor
1000 Manuscript Way
Anytown, USA 11223
566-1987

One of the first copyediting jobs I handled on a freelance basis was for an elderly gentleman who lived in my mother's apartment complex. He had been working on the same fantasy novel for ten or fifteen years. And while his novel definitely needed editing, he also just needed someone to talk to. For me, it was a great situation because he was able to pay me well (this was 20 years ago, and he paid me $12 an hour back then!). We went through two rounds of editing, and by the end of it all we were great friends and kept in touch for years afterwards.

On the other hand, I have met authors over the years who I would never consider working for. One of them was referred to me by a friend. He dropped his manuscript off at my house and asked me to read it. The book was a detective story, very violent and very badly written. The author had quit his job and spent an entire year working on his book, fully expecting to sell it to a publisher. But he had never taken a writing class in his life and had never had anyone read his manuscript before. Was he in for a rude awakening!

I passed on this job for three reasons: the author had absolutely no idea about what the publishing world was really like; the book needed so much work that he would practically have to start over; and the book was so violent that I couldn't stand reading it.

So, if you want to work with authors on a freelance basis, my advice to you is this: only work for authors you genuinely like as people; stick with authors who have some idea of how the publishing world works; and finally, only work for authors who can pay you enough to make it worth your while.

Training Opportunities

Classes in editing and English usage are often available through your local community college or adult education program. If you're really serious about becoming a copyeditor, I recommend the correspondence classes offered by the U.S. Department of Agriculture. They offer courses in editorial practices which include:

- Introduction to the Editing Process
- Intermediate Editing
- Printing, Layout, and Design
- Advanced Practice in Editing
- Technical Editing
- Introduction to On-Line Communications
- Publishing Management

Not only can you take individual classes, but if you take a series of classes you can earn one of four Certificates of Accomplishment: Editorial Practices, Technical Editorial Practices, Editorial Management, or Professional Editor. A certificate of accomplishment counselor is available by appointment. Call 202/720-5885 for more information.

For the Love of Words

Copyeditors are united by one thing above all else: a love of words, and of working with words for a living. If you really love what you're doing, other people will be able to tell—and your work will show it, too.

There are many niches in the copyediting world—from magazines, newspapers, and book publishers to technical publications and trade publications (some of them are listed in the back of this book). So if you want to give copyediting a try, give it everything you've got—knowing that you're sure to find a place in this exciting field!

Chapter 6: Indexing

Indexers are the unsung heroes of the nonfiction book world. A good indexer can save a so-so book from total oblivion. Think about it for a second — what good is a book about insects or stars if you can't find the page about bumblebees or the Big Dipper? It's a fact — with nonfiction books, more people turn to the index first than to the table of contents!

Make no mistake about it, indexing is an art form all its own. The good news is, it's easy to learn — and it can be very rewarding financially! Nowadays, there are many computer programs to help indexers with their job, too. And the opportunities are virtually unlimited — just about every nonfiction book that's worth the paper it's printed on has an index! That's tens of thousands of books every year, just waiting for indexers like yourself!

If you thrive on attention to detail and you are patient and thorough, you have the right temperament to be a successful indexer. Once you get established, the book world will be your oyster! This chapter will introduce you to this great field and tell you everything you need to know to get started.

The Basics of Indexing

Indexing is a job that comes at the very end of the publishing process. It's the last job to be completed before the printer starts rolling books off the press. In fact, when an indexer gets hold of a book project, the printing process has already begun. Indexers are given page proofs of the finished book so that the page numbers can be noted properly in the index.

Now, the printer usually has the printing of any one book scheduled up to six months in advance — but like so many things in life, usually unforeseen delays tend to push the schedule to the limit. So if the book is late getting to the indexer, it's up to the indexer to save the day and get the job done in record time!

More often than not, indexers find themselves trying to beat the clock. Editors tend to trust their indexers completely and often do not even check their work. Everything just gets shipped off to the printer as soon as possible! So, you can see why a trusted indexer is so important to a publishing house.

Indexers are almost always hired on a freelance basis. They know their publishers well and get hired over and over again. It's like having the security of a regular job without having to trudge into the office every day! No doubt about it, indexing is the perfect job to do from home. And though you'll work hard when there's a deadline to meet, you can set your own hours and enjoy the freedom that comes with the territory. And with rates ranging from $15 to $40 an hour, you can find your own niche and make as much money as you want!

Where to Learn the Trade

Believe it or not, one of the main ways indexers learn the trade in this country is through correspondence courses sponsored by the United States Department of Agriculture. Yes, it's true! You can take a course in Basic Indexing that will not only teach you the tricks of the trade, but will also introduce you to the business of freelance indexing.

The Basic Indexing course consists of 11 lessons — and because it's a correspondence course, you do it at your own pace, in the comfort of your own home. The USDA teaches the method of indexing used by the University of Chicago Press. To see what this method involves before you actually sign up for the course, take a look at the *Chicago Manual of Style*, 14th Edition — available at your local library or bookstore. There's a big section in this book on indexing that will be very helpful to you.

The USDA offers a second course called Applied Indexing, which you can take after you've completed the Basic Indexing course. In Applied Indexing, you actually create indexes for sections of eight different books. You also learn even more about how to run your own indexing business — everything from estimating the time it takes to complete an index to submitting your invoices.

The Basic Indexing course costs $281, and the Applied Indexing course costs $275. Since these two courses are all the training you need, we think this is one of the best deals around! For more information, write to:

The Graduate School of the U.S. Dept. of Agriculture
Correspondence Study Program
Room 1114, South Agriculture Building
14th and Independence Ave. SW
Washington, DC 20250

You can obtain a FREE catalog of the correspondence courses available through the U.S. Dept. of Agriculture by calling (202) 720-7123.

Another way to become an indexer is to get specialized training through a Library Science Program at a college or university near you. Some Library Science Programs will allow outsiders to audit their indexing courses. Make a phone call to your local college and find out if they offer a Library Science program. Then ask if it is possible for you to audit their indexing classes without enrolling in the entire two-year degree program. If there's a college near you with a good Library Science program, by all means investigate it; but we think the USDA courses are hard to beat!

Computerized Indexing

At this point you may be saying, "Wait a minute. I know that my computer's word processing program has an indexing feature. Why isn't that enough?"

It's definitely true that many computer programs, from Word Perfect to Microsoft Word and even Pagemaker, have indexing features. The problem is, they just aren't good enough. No one has come up with a computer program that completely replaces the work of a trained indexer. That's why publishers are willing to pay you so well if you're one of the smart ones who goes out and gets the training!

That said, professional indexers do use special computer software to help out with their work. This indexing software has the ability to sort and merge tens of thousands of entries automatically — it's as different from word processing as the space ship *Enterprise* is from a horse and buggy. The two main programs in use today are Macrex and Cindex, both out of Great Britain with distributors here in the U.S.

Macrex is the easiest to learn; it has menus like Windows or the Mac so you don't have to memorize a whole slew of commands. Among other things, Macrex offers a back-up file so editors can check the indexer's work; it also has the ability to take the index right into typesetting mode for the printer. For more information, write Macrex at the following address: Macrex, Wise Bytes, PO Box 3051, Daly City, CA 94015.

The America Online Writers Forum

If you've got a home computer and you're already a member of America Online, go to the Professions & Organizations menu and check out the Writer's Forum! There's a message board here called Editing/Indexing/Translating where you can exchange e-mail with other indexers. Topics include general discussions on the art of indexing, plus forums on the Cindex and Macrex computer programs we mentioned in the last section. There's even a "Who's Who of Indexers," where you can meet other like-minded individuals, both new and experienced.

This is a great way to learn more about indexing for very little money. You can pick up tips here and ask any questions you might have about the profession, knowing that you'll get answers from people who've really "been there and done that!"

Where's the Instruction Book?

Indexing jobs usually don't come with instructions. A publisher might tell you about any space limitations that will restrict the number of entries you can create; but more often, the editor will just say, "Index this book to the level you think is required." Sometimes the author will get involved and give instructions about what he or she wants indexed in the form of written notes passed on to you.

This lack of instruction is why you must get your training as an indexer elsewhere, like through the USDA courses described in this chapter. In most cases, the publisher just wants to hand you the assignment and let you run with it!

Indexed entries are usually measured "per page" of the finished book. For an average work of nonfiction, each page may have three to five entries in the index; a specialized book like a medical, legal, or engineering textbook may have up to 15 index entries per page.

So as you can imagine with all these entries, indexers do much more than simply search for key words! A real professional will design the index to guide readers to all references on a certain topic, idea, name, place or person — which means the indexer must understand the concepts as well as the facts. It helps if you have a flexible mind and love paying attention to details!

Here's a rule of thumb: an average 300-page book will probably require an index of between six and 15 pages in the finished book (that's assuming two columns on each page). It should take you between one and two weeks to complete an index of this size.

Questions of Style

Generally indexers follow one of these formats in preparing an index:

- A paragraph style where subentries appear right after the main entry in block formation;

- A main entry followed by indented subheadings on separate lines in alphabetical order.

The *Chicago Manual of Style*, 14th edition is one of the bibles of this industry. This book gives you the basics of how to go about creating index entries, how to alphabetize them, and how to prepare your finished index for submission to the publisher. You'll find it at larger bookstores and at your public library.

How to Break In

To get hired as an indexer, you usually have to send a letter with samples, called "tearsheets," from previous indexing jobs to the publisher of your choice. If you've never indexed a book before, then take the USDA "Applied Indexing" course and send in one of the sample indexes you write as part of their curriculum.

It can also be helpful if you have a specialized background that applies to certain types of books. Maybe you used to work in a law office or a doctor's office, or maybe you have picked up an expert's knowledge of gardening or even race cars over the years. It doesn't matter what the subject is — if you know all about it, and can find a publisher who publishes books about it, then YOU can shine as a star indexer!

Start with the list of publishers in Volume II. Then go to *Writer's Market* or the *Literary Market Place* at your local library and find out exactly what kind of nonfiction books these firms publish. The small amount of time this research takes will pay off in big dividends for you later! Only write those publishers that have a line of books where you think you could fit in well — and concentrate on publishers in your immediate area so that when they call, you can go in for an interview. Be selective, and you will increase your chances of success.

Here is a sample letter you can use as a starting point to approach a publisher about opportunities in indexing:

Today's Date

Bob Bigshot, Editor
SuperDuper Publishing Company
1 Success Way
Any City, USA

Dear Bob Bigshot:

I am very impressed with your firm's line of home medical guides. Having worked as a nurse practitioner for the past 15 years, I believe I can say with authority that your guides are among the best I have seen anywhere.

I am writing to inquire whether you have openings for freelance book indexers. I feel that with my medical background, I can successfully index books such as those that appear in your home medical line.

I have completed the USDA Basic Indexing and Applied Indexing courses; a sample of my work is enclosed. Please contact me at the address and phone number listed below if you are able to try me out on an indexing project. Thank you for your consideration.

Sincerely,

(signature)

Irma Indexer
555 Second St.
Anytown, USA 44556
344-6677

Growing Your Business

As we said earlier in this chapter, most indexers are freelancers. People just starting out in this field usually keep their regular jobs and do indexing part-time until they get the reputation they need to support full-time work.

As you gain confidence and experience, you'll find yourself getting many referrals. Editors at different publishing houses call each other to get referrals for good indexers. You will probably end up with two or three publishing houses that use you on a regular basis. Or, you may find one publishing house that wants to keep you all to themselves!

Most indexers work independently on a per book basis, but in the case of encyclopedias or extremely complex textbooks, several indexers may work as a team under the supervision of an editor. This type of situation can be good for beginning indexers, since there are plenty of other people around to learn from and help you out while you learn the ropes!

Bringing Home the Bacon

Indexers are generally paid by the hour or a fixed amount per every page in a book that has to be indexed. A typical rate is $3 per indexable page. Using our previous example of a 300-page book, let's say that only 250 of those pages actually need to be indexed. A little quick math will tell you that 250 times $3 per page equals $750 — not bad for a week's work! At that rate, you can work just eleven months of the year, take a month off, and still bring home $33,000!

Hourly rates start at around $12–15 per hour for beginners and go all the way up to $30–$40 per hour for indexers of highly specialized technical books in the medical, legal, and engineering fields.

Join the Pros

The American Society of Indexers (ASI) is the place you want to be! This organization offers many benefits to its members, including a magazine called *Key Words* that comes out six times a year. The magazine features articles on the current state of indexing, market services, reviews of indexing programs, and other topics of interest to indexers. Every year the ASI presents the H. W. Wilson Award for Excellence in Book Indexing to the best book indexer for that year.

The ASI also puts on a two-day annual conference, usually in May or June, in various cities throughout the United States. At this event you can meet between 100 and 250 working professionals in the field and take workshops to improve your skills.

For membership information and details about the annual conference, contact the American Society of Indexers by writing ASI, P.O. Box 386, Port Aransas, Texas 78373.

Indexing: The Final Frontier

While you may never have thought of indexing as a job opportunity, we hope that by now you can see the light! Indexing is definitely one of the best paying opportunities you can find as a freelancer in the publishing world. Plus, you can make a very real contribution to the success of a book with a good index.

A book with a good index is prized by librarians and will have a much longer shelf life than a book without an index. Most people know what they're looking for in a book, and if they can't find it in the index, they'll move on to another book that's more user-friendly.

According to one insider we talked to, a nonfiction book without an index represents "complete laziness on the part of the publisher!" A good book with a bad index will never reach its full potential, in terms of either sales or usefulness. On the other hand, a good index can make a bad book outstanding!

So there you have it — an indexer not only has a fascinating job, but provides one of the key ingredients of a book's success! This information in this chapter can help you realize your full potential in this wide-open field. Just remember, nothing ventured, nothing gained — so don't delay, explore your future as an indexer today!

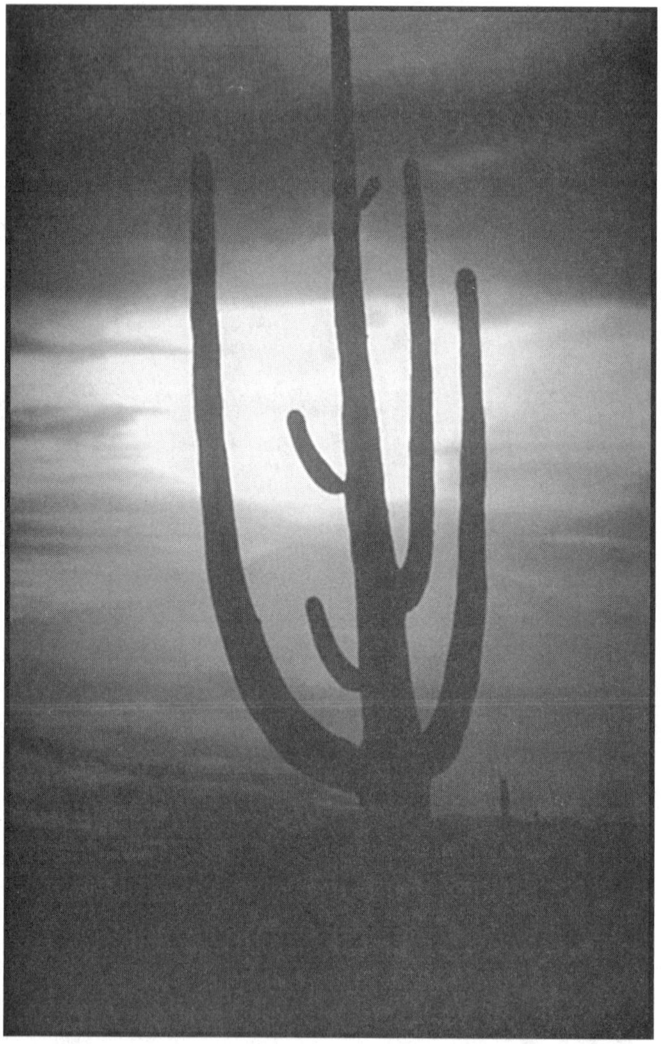

Chapter 7: Be a Fact Checker

Behind the scenes at most major magazines and publishing houses dwells a resident genius known as the fact checker. Actually, you don't have to be a genius to be a fact checker. If you pride yourself on attention to detail and love researching a wide variety of topics, you could find yourself in great demand in this little-known corner of the publishing world!

A fact checker guards the reputation of a publisher and its writers by guaranteeing that all the facts presented in a given piece of writing are correct. This is a complicated trade, one that can be more difficult than meets the eye. Even a seemingly simple fact can turn out to be fairly complex. For example, say you have to verify the year of someone's birth. What if there are conflicting records — and what if the person is so vain that they've lied about their age for the past twenty years?

You get the idea. Fact checkers deal with all kinds of situations like this, from confirming dates to describing complicated court decisions. Some publications — most notably, the magazine *The New Yorker* — take great pride in their fact checkers. Their goal is never to print a retraction — meaning, a correction of something that got into print that was incorrect. As far as I know, they've managed to keep a virtually spotless record for decades!

Fact checkers work either as freelancers or as in-house employees of magazines and publishing companies. Read on to learn how fact checking is done and decide whether it's the kind of work that will make you bound out of bed in the morning, bright-eyed and bushy-tailed!

What is a Fact?

Before we go any further, we must answer this seemingly simple question. What is a fact and how exactly do fact checkers ascertain which facts need to be researched and which don't? How do fact checkers learn to distinguish between a statement of fact and a disguised opinion?

The beginning fact checker is generally asked to underline in red all facts that he or she feels must be checked. The checker will then sit down with a senior checker or an editor who will then tell them if they were correct in their assumptions and give feedback on the spot — for example, "Check this fact that you didn't mark and don't bother checking this one that you did mark."

There is no school that will offer you training as a fact checker. Fact checkers learn by doing with constant consultation and supervision on the job, backed by policy safeguards set up by a publisher or magazine.

Obviously, mentoring by senior staff people is an essential to the care and training of a fact checker. Especially in the beginning, it helps to be in close proximity to other fact checkers (or at least an editor) so that you can compare notes with others and receive help and suggestions (the name of an expert to call, etc.). You might start out by working in the office, and then as you gain experience and confidence move to working from home. In any case, it doesn't take long for fact checkers to learn the basics, handle new terminology and navigate the waters of a particular publisher's attitude and relationship to the printed word.

Getting the Facts Straight

To evaluate the various and sundry facts that present themselves as a daily challenge, fact checkers rely on a four-tiered system of information sources. These four sources are described below.

1. Reference Books

Fact checkers often work in a library-like setting, surrounded by shelf after shelf of standard reference books (*Oxford English Dictionary*, *National Geographic Atlas*, etc.) plus many more specialty books in specific subject areas— not to mention a generous supply of relatively obscure reference books. Fact checkers at certain publishers will also rely on video information from television shows (political speeches, for example), movies, and other taped sources.

Magazines and publishers are committed to keeping their reference volumes up-to-date, and usually insist that the fact checker use them on site, even if you are a freelancer. You can get around this, though, because more and more standard and specialty reference works are available on CD-ROM or on-line via computer. (See number 3 below for details.)

2. Phone Contacts

If a source cannot be readily confirmed by reference books, fact checkers will use phone contacts that they have worked hard to develop and cultivate. These contacts are usually experts in their given fields. They are individuals who have proven their worth over time, and who can be relied upon implicitly to give the fact checker up-to-date and accurate information.

One of the most interesting aspects of being a fact checker is the getting to know these subject matter experts. They can be extremely fascinating people, as well as being helpful to you — plus you have the satisfaction of knowing that your people skills are responsible for maintaining these relationships and making it all happen!

3. Going On-Line

The recent boom in computer databases and on-line information services is the best thing that's happened to fact checkers in a hundred years! The NEXUS computer system is one of the most popular systems used by fact checkers, but there are literally hundreds of databases to choose from. Even the most popular on-line services like Prodigy, America Online and Compuserve are worth their weight in gold to fact checkers.

Using computer databases, you can call up vast treasure troves of information on a specific subject area. Yet another way to access huge amounts of data in a matter of seconds is CD-ROM discs. Most standard reference works, such as the *Oxford English Dictionary,* are available on CD-ROM. There's literally no need for a fact checker to sit hunched over in a library poring through volume after ancient volume — not any more! The computer allows you to call up the information you need with the touch of a button.

See Chapter 10, "Doing Research for Authors," for more information about databases and how you can put the Information Age to work for you.

4. Working with Writers

Contrary to what you might think, fact checkers are not out to prove that writers are wrong. Most fact checkers work together with the writer of a piece to review a manuscript — and this is especially true if it's a subject that the fact checker knows nothing about.

Obviously, the writer can be expected to know a lot about the subject at hand, since he or she has done the research necessary to write the piece. Writers can help out by referring the fact checker to various reference materials, including earlier articles or books on the same subject. Writers can also recommend knowledgeable subject experts with whom the fact checker can confer over the phone.

Most writers are extremely grateful to responsible fact checkers. Whether it's a typo or an oversight by the writer in the course of his research, sometimes all it takes is the conscientious eye of the fact checker to save a serious error from making its way into print!

Job Qualifications

You don't need an advanced college degree or experience in journalism in order to be a fact checker. Usually any kind of liberal arts degree will do. If you are familiar with a second modern language like French, Italian, German or Spanish, that's a plus. In addition to general aptitude and a broad educational background, you need a temperament that thrills to the chase, a highly developed sense of curiosity, and the drive to solve problems, however difficult and obscure.

Who Hires Fact Checkers?

Most national magazines that have reputations for good journalism employ one or more fact checkers, either on staff or on a freelance basis. It often happens that a freelancer can be kept so busy by a publisher that it's almost like working full time for them!

On the other hand, most newspapers do not hire fact checkers. With the time pressure of daily deadlines, it just isn't possible to use fact checkers — there isn't enough time. At the most, a reporter will run down to the in-house library or get the newspaper's own in-house librarian to check something out for them.

Some book publishers hire fact checkers to work in the nonfiction department, while other publishers may use a copyeditor instead who checks for facts as well as spelling, grammar, and matters of style. If there is no fact checker on staff, book publishers may hire freelancers or subject matter experts to check certain manuscripts. Sometimes, because works of nonfiction are usually written by a person who knows a subject well, publishers just say no to fact checking.

How to Get Hired

If fact checking appeals to you and you meet the personality profile described earlier in this chapter, start by contacting the offices of all the magazines located in your area. Make an initial phone call to each magazine and say, "I wonder if you could tell me the name and title of the person who's in charge of hiring fact checkers? I'm writing a letter and I need to know who to address it to." Then, once you have that information, send off a letter like the one below. Be sure to emphasize any experience you have that might be relevant to each particular magazine.

Today's Date

Annie Awesome, Editor
Anytown Travel Magazine
890 Profit St.
Anytown, USA 68790

Dear Annie:

I'm aware that you sometimes hire fact checkers on either an in-house or freelance basis. I would appreciate it very much if you would place my letter and resume on file for this purpose.

As you will note from my resume, I am attending night classes in English and French at Anytown Community College. I also have a special interest in travel, with experience working for a local travel agent as well as travel to England and France.

Would it be possible for me to fact check a sample manuscript so that you can evaluate my skills? If so, please contact me at the address and phone below.

Sincerely,

(signature)

Rebecca Reader
567 Park St.
Anytown, USA 45678
(901) 234-5678

After you send your letter, follow up a week to 10 days later with a phone call. When you call, ask for the editor or staff person you sent the letter to. Be very polite and professional, and say something like this: "I'm calling to follow up on a letter I sent you last week about fact checking. I'd like to know if you have any openings for fact checkers right now. If so, could I come in for an interview?" If the response is no, remain very courteous and ask if you could check back in a month or two in case their needs have changed. With a positive attitude and a little persistence, you will soon get yourself hired!

The pay for fact checking varies according to the publisher involved and the method used. If you're hired on a full or part-time basis by a magazine, you can expect to make $8 to $9 an hour to start, moving up to $12 an hour over time. Once you're an experienced fact checker, you can charge more if people know and trust you. If you have your own computer at home with access to various databases in specialized subject areas, you can make $20 an hour or more.

The more specialized you are, the more money you can make. Keep this in mind when evaluating your opportunities in the field of fact checking. For example, maybe you have experience in the medical field as a nurse, transcriptionist, office manager, or whatever. You might be able to find a medical magazine or a publisher of medical books who could really use someone with your special knowledge to fact check very specialized manuscripts.

The other good news is, even if you start out at the very lowest end of the scale, you really can move up to a bigger and better job, particularly in the magazine publishing world. We know of one woman who started out as an intern at a travel magazine while she was still a student. The editors trained her as a fact checker. She then moved up to become a researcher, and today she is an associate editor at the same magazine where she started out! Now, associate editor is a very high-ranking title, third from the top on the masthead of the magazine. The whole process only took her about seven years from start to finish. Now she's pulling down close to $40,000 a year, plus she has the added benefit of all expenses paid travel to exotic destinations around the world!

Chapter 8:
Writing Blurbs and Flap Copy

Have you ever picked up a book in a bookstore, read what it says on the back cover or the flap, and thought to yourself, "I have to buy this book!" At one time or another, this experience has happened to most of us who love books and reading. The copy on the back cover of a book is called a "blurb," and you too can learn the art of writing a good blurb and flap copy — words that will make people run up to the cash register and then run home to start reading the fascinating book you've described!

While some publishers have editorial assistants on staff whose duties include writing blurbs and flap copy, there are a great many publishers who hire freelancers to perform this task. A friend of mine named Sherry found a steady source of work writing blurbs for a publisher of reference books on all kinds of fascinating topics—from American women scientists to African political figures! Samples of her blurbs and flap copy appear later in this chapter.

Keep in mind that EVERY book has a blurb on its back cover, and EVERY hardcover book has copy on the flaps. The opportunities here are truly unlimited! Here's how the process of writing blurb and flap copy works.

Background Materials

You need some basic background materials about the book in order to write blurb and flap copy. The publisher will provide you with these materials at the time you start the job. They usually include:

- A complete copy of the book manuscript.

- A publisher's summary — which is a form filled out by the author of the book or the publisher — that describes what the book is about. This will usually summarize the plot or the table of contents, as well as describe who the intended audience is for the book.

- A copy of the publisher's guidelines for writing blurbs and flap copy. These guidelines will tell you how long your blurb or flap copy needs to be, and list any other information that must appear — such as the ISBN number and a credit line for the cover photo or artwork.

Not all publishers have written guidelines. If they don't, ask to see samples of books they've already published so that you can study how the blurbs are written. With some samples in hand and a copy of the book manuscript, you'll be all set to write!

The Art of Writing Blurbs

The average length of a book blurb is between 100 and 250 words. That's one page or less of double-spaced, typed copy! When you think about it, that's not very many words to get a potential reader excited about buying the book. As a blurb writer, that's your challenge — to convey what makes the book interesting in a small amount of space.

Once you have the publisher's background materials in hand, here's how you go about writing the blurb:

- Read the author's or publisher's summary, if there is one. Then SKIM the book manuscript, chapter by chapter. Don't read every word — unless you just can't put the book down and want to read it for your own enjoyment! Instead, read the first page and last page of every chapter, and quickly flip through the pages in between. This will give you a good "feel" for what the book is about.

- Ask yourself the following questions: what makes this book unique? If it is a nonfiction book, what can the reader expect to learn by reading it? If it is a fiction book, what kind of experience does it offer the reader? Make notes to yourself as you answer these questions.

- Chapter by chapter, make yourself a list of the high points of the book. You'll only have room for a handful of these in the blurb, but by making this list, you'll be able to see them at a glance and decide which ones are the most important.

- Read the publisher's guidelines for blurb writing. Does the publisher require a headline for the blurb, or do you simply use the title of the book as the headline? If it's a nonfiction book, does the publisher ask for examples of the contents to be included in the blurb? If it's a fiction book, what can you say about the plot that will catch the attention of a potential reader?

- Does the book have special features—for example, lots of photographs or diagrams, or a big reference section in the back? If so, you will probably want to mention this in your blurb.

- Is the author an expert in their field, or has the author written another book (or books) that should be mentioned in the blurb? Usually the author is only mentioned in the blurb if they are especially famous. The flap copy, which we'll discuss later in this chapter, describes the author of a book in more detail.

- Who can benefit from reading this book? Try to say something that describes the intended audience for the book in your blurb. This is especially true of nonfiction books.

Once you get the hang of blurb-writing, it should take you about two to three hours to write a really good blurb. The pay for this kind of work is in the $50-$75 range. See the next page for samples of two different kinds of blurbs.

Sample Blurb #1: Garden Book

Here's a blurb that appeared on a large coffee table book about the gardens of Santa Barbara, California. No headline appears with this blurb. The back cover was mostly taken up by a large photograph, with this text added to entice a reader to open up the volume and turn the pages:

> Nestled between Southern California's Santa Ynez Mountains and the Pacific Ocean, Santa Barbara has long been renowned as an oasis of spectacular gardens. From the grand estates of yesteryear to a multitude of contemporary showplaces, here the art of gardening is expressed in limitless diversity. *Santa Barbara, A California Paradise*, is the first book exclusively devoted to exploring these glorious gardens.
>
> Over two hundred and seventy-five color photographs display the full range of mastery of garden design in this paradise on Earth. A delight for gardeners and lovers of beauty everywhere!

Sample Blurb #2: Women Scientists Book

This much longer blurb gives specific examples of what the reader will find in the book. Note that the title of the book is used as the headline. This publisher obviously has very different requirements than the publisher of the garden book!

American Women Scientists: A Biographical Dictionary

American women scientists were unsung pioneers during the late nineteenth and early twentieth centuries. Outnumbered by their male peers and constrained by limited opportunities for education and travel, their contributions to the profession went largely unnoticed, despite their unparalleled record of achievement.

This ground-breaking biographical dictionary sets the record straight, with 400 profiles of noteworthy women scientists who began their careers prior to 1950. A few of these women, anthropologist Margaret Mead, for example, have reputations that transcend their fields; however, most are known for their work in a specific subject area. Discover women such as:

- Jane Colden, recognized as the first American woman botanist, who worked with her father preparing descriptions and taking botanical impressions

- Gladys Emerson, a nutritionist and biochemist who was a co-isolator of Vitamin E

- Barbara McClintock, a geneticist who won the Nobel prize for her pioneering work on the mechanism of genetic inheritance

- Annie Peck, an archaeologist and renowned explorer who was the first person to climb several mountains in the Peruvian Andes

- Ellen Richards, a chemist who was the first female science student and first female faculty member at the Massachusetts Institute of Technology

- Lucille Stickel, a zoologist who developed original methods for determining pesticide residue levels in wildlife

All biographies are indexed by profession, name, and subject, making this reference book eminently useful to scholars and instantly accessible to the interested lay person. A fascinating compilation, this volume is destined to become a classic and an inspiration to all those interested in women's contributions to science.

Use the Bookstore as Your Classroom

Give yourself a course in blurb writing by visiting your local bookstore. Pick up different kinds of books and read the blurbs. You'll discover many different styles of blurbs. Try writing a few of your own as practice. And while you're at it, read the flap copy of those books as well! Which brings us to our next section—

Writing Flap Copy

"Flap" copy appears on front and back flaps of hardcover books. The flaps are part of what is called the "dust jacket," which is the colorful printed wrapping that folds over the book's hard, permanent cover.

When you open up a hardcover book, the front flap is the first thing you see. No doubt about it, the flap copy is very important! It gives the potential reader a closer look at what he or she can expect from the volume within.

Flap copy generally ranges in length from 300 to 500 words —which is about twice as long as blurb copy. Most often the flap copy extends onto the back flap as well. Also, the back flap usually includes a brief biography about the author of the book, which may be accompanied by a photo.

If someone is browsing through the bookstore and is interested by the blurb copy on the back cover, they may decide to open up the book and read the flap copy. The flap copy is the second step to selling the book. It should give a more detailed look at the purpose or plot of the book, and tell what the reader can expect to gain by reading it.

Chapter 8: Writing Blurbs and Flap Copy 89

To summarize, flap copy usually includes the following:

- A detailed description of the contents of the book. The flap copy should give the reader a clear idea of the book's scope and purpose.

- A brief author biography. This may be a sentence or two, or longer if the publisher requires it. If the book uses photographers or illustrators, they may be profiled here as well. Check with the publisher if you're not sure who to include.

Writing flap copy requires the same basic background materials as writing blurbs: a copy of the manuscript, a copy of the publisher's book summary, and the publisher's style guide. Don't forget to ask for sample books from the publisher so you can imitate the style of flap copy they want.

Go to the bookstore and read book flaps there to get you "in the groove." Then take the dust jackets off a few of your books at home and practice writing flap copy for them. Compare your final results with what's on the publisher's dust jacket. How did you do?

Here's the flap copy that goes with each of the back cover blurbs used as examples earlier in this chapter.

Sample Flap Copy #1: Garden Book

Front Flap:

(Notice how the front flap copy expands on the information in the blurb and describes the contents of the book in more detail.)

> Along the Southern California coastline just one hundred miles north of Los Angeles, a fertile, tree-shaded enclave known as Santa Barbara rests at the base of the Santa Ynez Mountains. Since the 1890s, this secluded paradise has been home to the finan-

cial elite, who marshaled their vast resources to transform the natural landscape with a diversity of garden design.

Today the reputation of Santa Barbara's gardens has spread the world over. From traditional Italian and Spanish gardens to contemporary "lifestyle" gardens replete with recreational amenities; from drought-tolerant desert gardens to charming French and English cottage-style displays; and from acres of meticulous lawns dotted with statuary to tiny "hidden treasure" gardens tucked behind stone walls and wrought-iron gates — Santa Barbara truly has something for everyone.

Generation after generation, local landscape architects have taken full advantage of the vast array of options afforded by Santa Barbara's sunny, temperate climate to create innovative expressions in garden design. Fifty of their finest creations are represented in this volume. In their variety and stunning beauty, they demonstrate the evolution of California landscape design and provide an exciting, inside glimpse of the ultimate Southern California lifestyle.

Garden Book Back flap:

There are so many contributors to this volume that the back flap shows you four examples of how to write brief biographies!

About the Contributors

xxx xxx, a horticulturist, was raised in Tahiti, where she developed an early interest in tropical plants. She has researched and visited gardens throughout North America and Europe.

xxx xxx is an award-winning writer and architectural photographer whose work has appeared in several books and national magazines.

xxx xxx specializes in architectural, landscape and corporate photography. He lives in Southern California.

xxx xxx is a landscape architect with more than twenty-five years experience. Her nationally acclaimed work has been featured in numerous magazines and books.

Sample Flap Copy #2: Women Scientists Book

Notice how this flap copy uses examples, statistics, and descriptions of women scientists to expand on the back cover blurb. A two-sentence author bio appears at the end. Obviously, the publisher considers the contents of this book to be more important than a description of the author!

American Women Scientists: A Biographical Dictionary

When xxx xxx informed a male colleague that she was preparing a historical encyclopedia on women scientists in America, he commented, "That should take all of two paragraphs." He was voicing a common misconception. The role of women in science during the nineteenth and early twentieth centuries has been consistently underestimated in the United States.

In fact, prior to 1950 American women scientists made significant contributions to most major fields of scientific endeavor. *American Women Scientists: A Biographical Dictionary* pays tribute to these pioneers, many of whom fought an uphill battle to gain education, career opportunities, and professional acceptance.

Concise biographies of 400 women of science are included in this exceptional volume; they chronicle a distinguished record of achievement, characterized by fierce independence, steadfast perseverance, and sheer brilliance. Among them are:

- Lucy Braun, a botanist who was instrumental in developing the scientific discipline of ecology in the United States

- Lillian Gilbreth, a founder of the discipline of scientific management, a pioneer in industrial psychology, and mother of twelve children

- Martha Maxwell, a self-employed taxidermist and owner of a natural history museum, and so well known that a Smithsonian ornithologist named a subspecies of owl in her honor

Entries include each woman's educational background, employment history, honors, and publications, and they place her achievements in the appropriate scientific and social context. The thoroughly researched encyclopedia is indexed by profession, name, and subject.

In the late twentieth century, one in four scientists is a woman, owing a tremendous debt to her predecessors who are honored in this volume. *American Women Scientists: A Biographical Dictionary* is an outstanding reference for students and teachers of women's studies and science, as well as anyone interested in the scientific achievements of women.

xxx xxx is Life Sciences Librarian at Purdue University Life Sciences Library. She has authored two other books and over twenty articles on a variety of topics.

How to Break In

The best way to find work writing book blurbs and flap copy is to start small and local. Are there writing classes in or near your town? Attend them and let the writers there know what you can do. Many writers publish their own books, and they need a friend who can provide an objective viewpoint to write the blurbs and flaps. You can also find writers know local publishers in person and can introduce you. (Plus, you get the added benefit of becoming a better writer yourself by attending the class!)

Once you've written a few blurbs and flaps, use them as samples to send to publishers near you. (See the list of publishers in Volume II.) Along with your samples, send a cover letter that reads something like this:

Today's Date

Josephine Jones, Marketing Director
XYZ Publishing
100 Main Street
Anytown, USA

Dear Ms. Jones:

I am writing to inquire if you have the need for experienced freelancers to write blurb and flap copy for your books.

I have written blurb and flap copy for books similar to those published by your company. Several samples of my work are enclosed.

My experience in publishing includes freelance work for ABC Press, a local publisher of children's books. I have a BA in English from Anytown Community College.

Please contact me at 123-4567 if you can use my services. I look forward to hearing from you.

Sincerely,

(signature)

Jane Doe
444 Market St.
Anytown, USA 67548

New Book Releases

Oftentimes publishers will ask the same person who writes the blurbs and flap copy for a book to write a "new book release." This is a press release that goes out to bookstores, magazines, newspapers, and other publications announcing the arrival of a new book.

The publisher will provide you with guidelines and samples for writing a new book release. Simply follow the format that they have provided. New book releases are usually one page long and contain the same type of information you've already provided in the blurb and flap copy.

If you get the opportunity to write a new book release, by all means do so! The work is easy, and it's more money in the bank for you — another $50–$75 worth. Always save a copy of what you write for your portfolio, and you'll be well on your way to getting even more great-paying work in the future!

Chapter 9: Writing Book Reviews

How about reading a good book, commenting on it in public, getting your name in print, and getting paid for it — not to mention keeping your free copy of the book? Is this called having your cake and eating it too? No, it's called book reviewing — and what could be better for a lover of reading?

Book reviewing has all these benefits, and more. One of the easiest ways to break into print as a published writer is to do book reviews for your local newspaper, club or company newsletters, or other publications in your community. And you don't need a college degree to write good book reviews. All you need is a love of reading and the ability to convey your opinions about a book in the short amount of space provided by a book review.

Getting Ready

Being well read in any one particular area — be it mysteries, crime fiction, romances, or any other form—will help you write good reviews. But the main thing to remember is that the best book reviews are individual and honest, with a distinct flavor of personal opinion — your audience wants to know what you think and why. There's simply no substitute for being able to tell it how you see it to whatever audience is reading your review!NEW PAGE 95

You might want to jump ahead and take a look at Chapter 18, "How To Read Critically," to review the skills that will help you embark on the exciting adventure of writing book reviews. This chapter will take you on an armchair journey of the basics you need to know before you begin. But rest assured that it won't be long before you see your very first review in print!

Join a Book Club

It never ceases to amaze me how many book clubs exist in my small city. By book club I don't mean a place where you order books by mail; instead, I mean small groups of 8–12 people who meet in someone's home once a month to discuss a book they've all read. Usually each member of the group gets to choose a book on a rotating basis.

There are no dues or membership fees for these groups; all you pay is the cost of the book you read each month, which are probably books you would have bought or borrowed at the library anyway!

As a beginning book reviewer, you can benefit tremendously from discussing books on a regular basis with like-minded people. You'll start to understand how many different reactions there can be to one and the same book. Some books you'll like and some books you won't, and you'll have the chance to share your opinions either way. Plus, you'll make some great friends in the process — people who will be only too willing to support you in your new career!

How do you find these private book clubs? The best way is by word of mouth. Ask your friends and inquire at your local bookstore. Read the classified ad sections of the newspaper. Call your local community college or Adult Education program. If you beat the bushes and don't come up with any book clubs, by all means, start your own! Invite a half a dozen friends to the first meeting. Set a time to meet once every month or once every two months. The meeting can rotate so it's held at a different member's house each time. Take a vote on what book you'll read first, or designate someone to make that decision. Serve some light refreshments and watch the enthusiasm take over!

Book Reviews Are Everywhere!

Just about every magazine and newspaper, from *People Magazine* to *USA Today*, has a book review section. (Even *Playboy* has book reviews, and very good ones too, we might add!) Take a look at the book reviews in the magazines or newspapers you usually read. Oftentimes your Sunday newspaper will have a special book review section, even if it's just a column or two. In larger newspapers like the *Los Angeles Times*, the *New York Times*, and the *Washington Post*, there's a separate section completely devoted to books. These sections can teach you a lot about the wonderful world of book reviews.

If you want to learn even more, you might go to your public library and read the reviews in *Library Journal* or *Publisher's Weekly*. These publications will give you a different perspective because they focus on a very important market: bookstore owners and other professional book buyers.

Get in the habit of clipping out your favorite book reviews and saving them in a file folder. What attracts your attention to a particular book review? Is it the reviewer's sense of humor, or how the reviewer compares the book at hand to other books that you've also read? Make a note of the strategies you like and try them out yourself in your own book reviews!

Another useful experiment is to collect reviews of the same book that have appeared in different publications. Try to find both favorable and unfavorable reviews. Then read the book yourself, if you haven't already, and compare your reaction to that of the published reviewers. How would you have reviewed the book differently? Next, write a review of the book yourself. We'll show you how later in this chapter.

The Inside Scoop

Insiders in the book publishing world are often able to read a Sunday book review section like someone else would watch a soap opera. They can tell which reviewers are scratching the backs of an author or publisher by writing a good review, as well as who is fighting who. Maybe someone else is trying to build a following for a point of view, whether it's political, moral, or otherwise. And maybe a professor who's up for tenure is trying to make a good impression by writing a flood of book reviews!

So book reviewing is just like any other profession or calling in life. Among book reviewers you'll find the good, the bad, the ugly, and everything in between. Sometimes the stakes are high in the book reviewing world because so many people want to write reviews. But you can beat them all to the punch and become the voice people count on to tell them about the latest good read — here's how!

How to Write Reviews

The basic idea of book reviewing is this: you want to intrigue the reader — and get them to buy the book! — but you must do this without giving away the whole story. If you either really love or really hate a book, be extra careful. Part of a reviewer's job is to present a fair assessment of the book. That means giving your own opinion, to be sure, but also leaving enough space for readers to form their own opinions as well.

In a way, writing a book review is like putting the book on trial — you want the book to remain innocent until proven guilty. In other words, you don't want your views to affect your readers so much that they can no longer form their own opinions. Every book deserves a fair trial. The reviewer is a stand-in for the reader and must take responsibility for potential readers of the book by not alienating them.

Every Book is Different

One experienced book reviewer we talked to says that there is no set blueprint or formula for writing a book review. He says that a review succeeds by reflecting the qualities of each particular book, along with the personality of the reviewer.

If you spend some time reading book reviews, we think you'll see that this is true. There are as many different kinds of book reviews as there are reviewers. Your job is simply to observe what's out there, learn from it, and then apply it in your own unique way.

Breaking Into Print

Below we'll describe several ways of breaking into print as a book reviewer. Keep in mind that your goal should be to write book reviews on a regular basis — whether it's once a month or once a week — especially when you're first starting out. This is definitely an area where practice makes perfect! The more reviews you write, the better they will be. Then your opportunities to be published — and your income — will expand accordingly!

Book Reviews for Newsletters

Do you belong to a club or organization that has a newsletter? Or do you work for a company that has an employee newsletter? These publications are great forums for your book reviews, especially when you're first starting out.

Remember, the idea is to get you and your name out there as a book reviewer. Your club or your company might not be able to pay you for writing book reviews, but look at it this way: once you've written a half a dozen reviews for the newsletter, then you have something to show the editors at magazines or newspapers. You've also become a much better book reviewer for the practice — and you've earned a reputation among your friends and colleagues for your efforts!

A good way to start out is by writing "mini" book reviews of one or two paragraphs each. It's easier for you, and newsletters usually have even less space than newspapers or magazines for book reviews. Start small, then work your way up to a longer review. Soon people you don't even know will be coming up to you, wanting to talk about your latest review. All that attention will help build your confidence and ensure your future success.

Reviewing Books for Newspapers

Most newspapers hire freelance book reviewers. Lots of times all you have to do is ask! Start out by calling your local newspaper and asking to speak to the editor in charge of book reviews.

When that person gets on the line, tell them that you are interested in writing book reviews on an ongoing basis and that you're willing to write a sample review as a trial run. If you are interested in reviewing books in a specific area — say children's books, or recent fiction — be sure to let the editor know that too.

If they don't need anyone at the moment, they will probably take your name and number and call you later when a book review slot opens up. If this doesn't happen, though, thank the editor politely for their time and ask if you can check back again in a month or two. Meanwhile, send the editor a thank you note and a sample book review that you've written. Be patient, and rest assured that soon you'll be seeing your name in print!

On the next page is a sample follow-up letter that you can use as a model for your own letter to send your home town newspaper editor. (P.S. Do NOT call editors at large newspapers or magazines—instead, send a query letter. See the sample query letter later in this chapter.)

Book Columns for Newspapers

Here's another idea that you can propose to your local newspaper: how about writing a book column that includes interviews with writers and publishers in addition to book reviews? A column like this gives you a much broader range of subjects to write about than book review after book review.

Today's Date

Eddie Editor
Anytown Gazette
345 Main St.
Anytown, USA

Dear Eddie Editor:

Thank you for speaking with me on the telephone today. As I promised, enclosed is a sample book review.

This review is about a new book called *Secrets of Successful Parenting*, which I feel is a topic especially important to both mothers and fathers in today's world. As a book reviewer, I am most interested in reviewing books about families and subjects of interest to families.

I have an AA degree from Anytown Community College in home economics, and I teach classes in homemaking at the Girls Club. The enclosed book review appeared in the Girls Club newsletter, where my book reviews are featured every month.

I would very much appreciate the opportunity to review books for the *Anytown Gazette*. Please let me know when an opening becomes available. Again, thank you for your time, and I look forward to hearing from you. You may reach me at 778-5000.

Sincerely,

(signature)

Joan Jones
456 Pleasant St.
Anytown, USA 12345

We know one writer who produces a column like this every week in the Sunday newspaper, and it's become something read by everyone in town who loves books! She specializes in reviewing books that have been written by people who live right in the community, though she reviews best sellers as well. Her column also lists all events related to books and publishing that take place around town every week — like book signings, workshops, and meetings of writer's organizations.

There's no better way to become recognized as an authority on publishing in your community than to start writing a column like this one!

Book Reviews for Magazines

There's an old saying we talk about elsewhere in this book that goes, "write about what you know." That statement applies to writing book reviews just as well as writing fiction or anything else.

Sometimes you can create a demand for yourself as a book reviewer if you are considered an expert in any field — whether it's race cars or crafts or movies or cooking. Just think about all the cookbooks that have been written, for example — and you can bet that those cookbooks are being reviewed in cooking magazines, as well as in other kinds of general interest magazines!

Which brings us to an important point. To get published as a book reviewer in magazines, seek out the magazines that exist in your area of interest. For cooking, it might be *Bon Appetit*, *Gourmet*, and home magazines like *Good Housekeeping*. Read their book reviews and become familiar with the styles in which they are written. Then you'll be ready to start writing reviews of your own!

Finding the Right Magazines

If you need help finding magazines in your area of interest, pay a visit to the biggest bookstore in your area and spend some time in the magazine section. For example, Barnes and Noble is a nationwide chain that is known for its huge magazine section. You'll probably find magazines there that you never knew existed — and chances are that nearly every single one of them will have book reviews.

Also, go to the periodicals room at your local library and do the same thing. Ask the reference librarian to help you locate a list of magazines in your subject area. You can also consult *Writer's Market* and *Writer's Digest Magazine*, which publish the names of magazines, their addresses, and the names of their editors — all of which are valuable information for you!

A word of warning: NEVER, EVER contact an editor at a magazine about writing book reviews — or about writing anything else, for that matter — unless you have actually seen a copy of the magazine first and read it carefully! Believe us, an editor will spot you coming a mile away if you have never read or seen their magazine — and they will shut the door in your face. If the magazine is not available at your local bookstore or library, send for a sample copy before you do anything else. Remember, you might not even LIKE the magazine after you've seen it — and you should ONLY write for magazines that you like and that you'd be proud to have your name printed in! So do yourself and the magazine a big favor and become familiar with the publication first and foremost!

Approaching the Magazines of Your Choice

If you are a subject expert who has never written a book review, find two recently published books in your field and write your own reviews. Then send these samples to editors at the magazines in your field, and tell them that these samples show how you would handle book review assignments.

Make sure you know the book editor's name for the query letter. Do not just send a letter "Attention Book Editor" if you can help it. Remember, you can find the editors' names in *Writer's Market*. If they aren't there, call the publication as a last resort and ask the receptionist for the right name. (Do not disturb the editors by speaking to them directly — letters are a far more effective way to break in. It will only take one experience of a busy editor hanging up on you to show you that this is true!)

If your query letter and sample reviews are interesting, an editor may give you a shot at a book review or several mini-reviews. If the magazine likes your work, they might consider hiring you to write reviews on a regular basis. The more you write, the more you can earn — and before you know it you'll have a following, perhaps extending to people all over the country!

Here's a sample query letter for a magazine that you can use to model your own:

Today's Date

Elizabeth Editor
Cooking With Gas
890 Lowfat Avenue
Any City, USA 00000

Dear Elizabeth Editor:

I've read *Cooking with Gas* since your very first issue, and I find that I use many of the recipes and tips every day. Thanks for producing a magazine I look forward to receiving every month!

I would like to inquire if you have the need for freelance book reviewers. My area of expertise is home economics and cooking, and I write book reviews every month for the Girls Club newsletter in Anytown. A sample review is enclosed.

I have an AA degree from Anytown Community College in home economics, and I teach classes in homemaking at the Girls Club. I have also taught classes in "Basic French Cooking" and "Cooking for One" through Anytown's Adult Education Program.

I would very much appreciate the opportunity to review books for *Cooking with Gas*. Please let me know when an opening becomes available. Again, thank you for your time, and I look forward to hearing from you. You can reach me at 313-558-4948.

Sincerely,

Joan Jones
456 Pleasant St.
Anytown, USA 12345

How Editors Assign Book Reviews

There are basically two ways editors assign book reviews. Some publications, like the *Los Angeles Times Book Review* for example, never let reviewers choose the books they want to review. They are afraid that reviewers won't be impartial enough if they only read books that they just love to death. Then again, other publications actually want requests from reviewers because they realize that good reviewers can help choose which books are worth writing about from all the hundreds they receive in the mail.

The first thing the editor will do is hand you a copy of the book they want you to review. You get to keep this copy — hurrah, your first big perk of the job! Then the editor will specify the number of words you are to write. A typical book review runs about 750 words — though some may be much longer, and mini-reviews will be 500 words or less. In longer reviews, remember that the last few paragraphs are always in danger of being cut if something more important has to fit in the publication instead—so always put the most important information in your review towards the beginning!

Writing the Review

You will usually have anywhere from one month to two weeks to complete your book review. Your first job, of course, is to read the book. As you read, keep a pencil in hand and make check marks in the margins every time something strikes you as being particularly important. (By using pencil, you can erase your check marks later if you want.)

Then, use these check marks to guide you as you look back over the book in preparation to write your review. On a separate sheet of paper, make a list of all the page numbers where you make check marks. Then, next to each page number, write just a sentence or two about what it was that caught your attention.

Once you've done this, your review has practically written itself! All you have to do is put your sentences in the right order and fill in a few gaps. You can use your page of notes almost exclusively, just going back to the book to write down a few quotes if you feel they are appropriate.

You're In the Money

In most cases, a freelance book reviewer is paid $50 to $100 per book review. This assumes the review falls somewhere around the standard length of 750 words. Longer reviews generally pay more, and shorter reviews may pay less — with the smallest, the mini-review, paying perhaps $35 per book. Remember, though, that a mini-review takes less time, since it's just a paragraph or two, and you will often be assigned more than one mini-review to do at once.

The good news is, no matter how long the review, you always get to keep the book. Plus, the longer you're around a publication, you'll probably get to take home copies of other books that never get reviewed. You'll be amazed once you see how many copies of books come pouring into the offices of magazines and newspapers all over the country — and most of them are never read OR reviewed!

As you make your way in the world of book reviewing, you'll be able to command more and more money. Book reviewers for the top magazines and newspapers in the country make $200 per review — sometimes even more!

Job Opportunities

Many publications have a stable of freelancers they use on a regular basis. Others have full-time book reviewers on staff. This is a popular field, but as one insider said, someone is always leaving the ranks for one reason or another. There is plenty of work out there for you — all you have to do is go and get it! Get known, get published, and you'll be amazed at the opportunities that come your way!

Chapter 10: Doing Research for Authors

There's a story in the annals of publishing, circa 1994/95, that is making researchers everywhere sit up and take notice — as well as drawing new people into the profession! It's a tale of generosity and unexpected good fortune that has already entered the hallowed halls of publishing history.

You've probably heard of *The Book of Virtues* by William Bennett. You might even have a copy of it in your house, since it's a very popular book and a *New York Times* best-seller. If you haven't seen it before, hightail it down to your local bookstore as soon as possible and take a look at it. As a budding researcher, you need to know about this book!

The story behind the book is this: the author, Bennett, hired a researcher to discover stories about virtuous people and events. This researcher traveled far and wide, all over the country, to search out material for the book. Then Bennett had a cash flow problem when it came time to pay the researcher. The two struck a deal. Instead of payment up front, the researcher would receive a percentage of all royalties from the sale of the book.

In a completely unexpected turn of events, the book became a huge hit. So what did the author do? The virtuous thing, of course. Bennett kept his pledge to the researcher, who literally made millions of dollars for his contribution. Now there are plans afoot for Bennett to write a sequel to *The Book of Virtues*, and guess what? He's already hired the same researcher, who will keep the same royalty split for the new book!

The publicity from this amazing turn of events is bringing public attention to that most obscure of jobs: the book researcher. To give you an insight into this profession, this chapter offers information about how to conduct research, information sources, and how to hook up with authors who need your services.

The Basics: Libraries and Reference Librarians

If you are lucky enough to live in a metropolitan area that supports a good-sized public library with a reference desk, you will have a "leg up" in the information search — and their services are free! If you have a college or university nearby, you might consider joining their library as well. Many university libraries offer community library cards for a yearly fee. Here's an inside tip: by joining the school's alumni organization (in many cases, you don't have to be an alumnus to join!) you can often get library privileges at a cheaper rate than the community library card.

If none of these options are available, consider developing a relationship with the reference desk at a library out of town. Some libraries will fax, copy and mail information to you as well as consult over the phone. All it takes is sincerity, courtesy, and respect on your part to establish a good long-distance relationship — you might make a visit to the library of your choice when you first start out, but then again we know researchers who've worked with librarians by phone for years! This is especially true of people who do research in obscure subject areas, where perhaps just a few libraries in the country have the special collections to meet their needs.

Make Friends With Your Librarian

Let's say you've found the library you want and need, whether it's around the corner or in the next state. Now's the time to start establishing good relationships there. It's always a good idea to make friends with the reference librarian — and with the whole library staff, for that matter!

Librarians are public servants with two years of postgraduate library school scholarship. They know how to find information on just about anything. That's their job — to help anyone who comes in or calls the reference desk by drawing on their vast store of expertise. In my experience, reference librarians are actually thrilled to help people out by providing accurate information on demand very quickly.

These days most public libraries have fully computerized card catalogs of their holdings, as well as the holdings of other nearby libraries within the same on-line system. Most libraries also have access to the other card catalogs by computer as well as on-line services in special research areas.

How To Proceed

Reference desks are often besieged all day long by schoolchildren and adults asking all kinds of questions. It pays to make a good impression. Whether you approach the reference librarian by phone or in person, be prepared. Know your questions and possible sources. Tell the reference librarian what you are doing. Librarians tend to tailor and deliver information based on how you ask your questions. The better prepared you are, the better the quality of information you will get!

If the reference desk is very busy or if your questions are complicated, the reference librarian might ask you to contact the desk at a certain time when it is less busy (a weekday morning, say) or the librarian may take your number and get back to you by phone.

Library Resources

In addition to computerized information and source checks, the reference librarian will have at hand a vast slew of reference materials and guides to help you. If necessary, the librarian will refer you to other libraries (Botanic, Natural History, Genealogy, University, etc.) as well as tell you who to talk to at each institution.

Reference librarians also know about community resources and all kinds of things not restricted to reference books. For example, they might be able to give you the phone number of an expert who could open the doors of your research wide open. My motto: when in doubt, ask the reference librarian!

You may receive the blue-ribbon treatment at certain reference desks. I have certainly found this to be true as I have been given valuable leads, names, and sources that were just what I needed — without my even knowing that this information existed!

One reference librarian told me about a researcher who called from out-of-town seeking information about a certain shipwreck. The librarian found the information, copied it and mailed it to the researcher — at no charge! Libraries are not always so generous with their time and money, but as a matter of public policy, most are. Your library is truly a resource of the first order!

Using Computers for Research

No doubt you've heard about the "Information Superhighway." While it's still hard to define, what it comes down to is that the amount of information available via computer is growing faster than you can say "Big Bang." In this exploding field, two popular computer services stand out as especially helpful for beginning researchers: America Online and Compuserve.

All you need to tap into these systems is a computer, a modem, and a telephone. The modem uses your phone line to establish a connection with the computer service. You pay so much a month for the basic service, plus a charge for how much time you spend on the computer.

America Online is the cheapest of them all, currently at $9.95 per month. Best of all, the software you need to sign on is free! Call America Online at 1-800-827-6364 and they'll send you everything you need to get started — and the first 10 hours you spend on-line are free, too! You can access forums and "rooms" to chat with like-minded folks, post questions, get answers, and generally wire yourself into the world at large.

When it comes to user forums, Compuserve is one of the best services around. There are literally hundreds of forums where you can chat with like-minded people. It's easy to get onto Compuserve, too. Just go down to your local bookstore — most bookstores sell the disks you need to get onto Compuserve. And while you're there, pick up a copy of *Compuserve from A-Z, The Ultimate Compuserve Reference* by Charles Bowen (Random House). It will help you learn the fine points of maneuvering around the system.

You can also get free disks to try America OnLine and Compuserve in computer magazines including *PC World, PC Magazine, Mac World,* and *Mac User.*

Dialog and Other Research Databases

The more experienced you get at doing research with your computer — and the bigger clients you get — the more money you'll have to invest in other on-line services. There are literally dozens of database services you can subscribe to. Some cover specific subject areas; others give you access to resources like newspapers in every major city. Some of these sophisticated reference services can be very expensive to use, so you need to be sure you'll really make good use of them before you sign up!

Just remember, the world of knowledge at your command is virtually infinite. For example, you can enter a single key word and these computer services will search for newspaper articles about that subject from all over the country — even the world! You can research the financial records of public companies (not to mention the resumes of their leaders), or find out about the latest medical research in a particular area, or just about anything else you want to know!

A really great thing about Compuserve is that it serves as a gateway to another database called Dialog. If you're really serious about doing research via computer, Dialog is where you want to be! It's the Queen Mother of databases, with over 600 of them on line. You can get national and international newspapers, including items like the *Tokyo Star* in English on a daily basis. Be forewarned, though, that Dialog doesn't come cheap: there's a hefty one-time sign-up fee, and then it costs anywhere from $3 to $20 for every article you download. But if you have a client who'll pick up the tab, this service can be worth its weight in gold!

More Research Databases

Here are three other databases you should know about:

- NewsNet: this service offers over 600 newsletters on-line, everything from the *Funeral Director Weekly* to pricey investment newsletters that you would never subscribe to on your own! You can search all 600 of these newsletters by key words to access information on the subject of your choice.

- Lexis/Nexis: this service is a competitor of Dialog, offering many of the same features. It's used by a lot of attorneys for legal research.

- Dow Jones News Retrieval: this service specializes in business journals, both foreign and domestic. It's also one of the more expensive services around — but it might be worth it to you if you have a big business client.

Start Off Quick with Kwik Knowledge

Is all this information about computer databases just too much for you? Beginners to the world of on-line information will love a user-friendly software package called Kwik Knowledge, which gives you easy access to the 120 databases on Compuserve known as Knowledge Index. Specifically, these databases include 34 major newspapers, the National Library of Medicine, Magill's Survey of Cinema (with articles on films dating back to 1902!), Standard and Poor's corporate profiles, business databases, and much more.

For more information about Kwik Knowledge, write Desktop Information at 32 W. Anapamu Suite 200, Santa Barbara, CA 93101. Send an SASE for information. Or, if you're already on Compuserve, you can contact Desktop Information at 75156,3024.

What About the Internet?

The Big Daddy of the Information Superhighway is the Internet. The Internet is different from America Online or Compuserve in that you can't just pop a disk in your home computer and suddenly be on the Net (though both of those services provide limited access to parts of the Internet). To explore the Internet in its entirety, you must gain access through a company or organization in your area that has a "node."

With the Internet, the world is truly at your fingertips. And while the Internet is truly daunting in size, you can rest assured that whatever subject you wish to research, you will find like-minded individuals and plenty of information here. If you think the Internet is for you, by all means take a class in how to use it. It's much too complicated for most folks to pick up on their own—though there are many books out these days to help you. Try *The Internet Yellow Pages* by Harley Hahn and Rick Stout (Osborne McGraw Hill), available at your local bookstore.

Here's a tip for Macintosh users: you can order an Internet Starter Kit from MacWarehouse for a mere $19.95 by calling 1-800-255-6227. This kit will show you how to hook onto networks all over the world, including universal e-mail and news services.

Information Brokers

If the information you need is complex or obscure, or if you're not able to access the information on-line yourself, you might consider contacting an information broker. These brokers are computer specialists trained in information search and retrieval.

There are currently several hundred information brokers in the country. Call their professional organization, The Association of Independent Information Professionals at (212) 779-1855 for referrals to information brokers in your area. One information broker we know charges $85 an hour or more for his sophisticated searches, so this is probably an option only if you're working for a writer or other client who has plenty of money to burn!

CD-ROM Discs

Even if you don't go on-line to do your research, you can take advantage of another great resource if you have a computer: CD-ROM discs. These discs look just like the CDs you buy in the music store, but instead of your favorite tunes, they store huge amounts of valuable information on just about every subject under the sun!

In order to use these CD-ROM discs, you need a special CD-ROM drive that hooks onto your computer. The cheapest CD-ROM drives start at around $100, and you can get a very good CD-ROM drive for around $200. The best deals on CD-ROM drives are in the computer mail-order magazines. You can call them toll-free at the numbers listed below and ask for a FREE copy of their catalog.

For Macintosh computers:
MacMall, 1-800-222-2808

MacConnection, 1-800-800-2222

TigerSoftware, 1-800-666-2562

MacWarehouse, 1-800-255-6227

For PCs (IBMs & IBM compatibles):
PC Connection, 1-800-800-5555

DellWare, 1-800-449-3355

All of these companies also carry full lines of CD-ROM discs. You can find reference sources like the entire Grolier Encyclopedia on a single CD-ROM! You can also find the complete atlas of the world, a street atlas for the entire United States, the American Heritage Dictionary, and Roget's Thesaurus, plus CD-ROMs on history, art, travel, languages, and much more!

Researching by Phone

When all's said and done about computers, you can do plenty of successful research with nothing more than a telephone. Many businesses, agencies, nonprofit organizations and other institutions, both public and private, have public relations people on staff and even 800 lines to deal with questions from the public. Brochures and other written materials, as well as on-line information services, are often available upon request for free or for a minimal fee.

Obviously some agencies will be more friendly than others. Nowadays lengthy phone menus sometimes make it difficult to get through to a real person, but you always can if you just persevere. Remember, public agencies have an obligation to honor your requests for information!

If you wish to speak to a particular person, that person's secretary or assistant may be protective and wary, especially if they don't know you. So to help you succeed in making cold calls to people you don't know, here are some tips from a veteran researcher:

- On the phone, act like you know the person you wish to speak to.

- Don't leave messages with underlings if you can help it. If you must, keep it brief. By all means, avoid leaving long messages!

- Persist in calling back until you reach the person you want directly.

- Be extra courteous at all times and address the assistants by name once you get to know them — as you will if you call back many times over!

Interviewing "Just Folks"

Interviewing ordinary people who aren't involved in the business world, the government or public life requires tact, compassion and the right approach. Such people are generally not trained to answer questions, and they may freeze up or even start talking about another subject.

As a researcher, you must gain the trust of the person you're interviewing. Do everything you can to put them at ease. Don't hide your purpose, but also don't put people on the spot. Let them tell their story in their own natural way. Use a tape recorder if at all possible — just put it on a table in front of you and act like it's not there. Soon the person you're speaking to will forget it's there, too. (You can also buy recording attachments for your phone—they're just a few dollars at a store like Radio Shack.)

Always make sure you date your research notes and tapes and keep them on file for easy retrieval. You never know when you'll be called upon to recontact certain sources or to reconfirm your research.

Questions To Ask Before You Begin

As a researcher, you may work either directly with an author or directly with a publisher. In either case, here are some questions to answer before you begin the work.

- Should the research be delivered in outline form, as raw notes, as prose, or as entire finished chapters?

- Should you provide the finished information on a computer disk as well as in printout form? (If they do want a computer disk, ask what kind of disk and what computer program they want you to use.)

- Exactly what kind of information is needed—answers to specific questions, or general information about a certain subject?

- Are there specific contact people or research sources to consult? Will you do the initial calls to set up interviews, or will the interviews be set up for you?

- As you conduct your research and contact people for interviews, how should you explain the relationship you have with the publisher or author, if at all? And how much can you reveal about the nature of the project?

- How will you check in with the author or publisher—by phone, fax, computer, or in person? And how often?

- What is the budget and the time frame for the research?

How to Find Work

In the publishing industry, there is no standard approach to hiring researchers. Publishing houses will use either freelance or in-house staff to provide the necessary research. The larger publishing houses may connect a good writer who knows nothing about a subject to a researcher who does.

Some publishers will direct their authors to experts in a given field to research certain books. Here's an example to get you going. Think of all the historical novels and romance novels that need accurate data on the clothes, habits, and manners of a certain era—whether it's the court of Louis XIV or the American frontier. Do you have a special interest in history? If so, and if you think this type of work might interest you, send a query letter to a publisher located near you who specializes in historical novels or romances. Consult the *Writer's Market* or *Literary Market Place* for lists of specific publishers. Here's a sample letter you can use as a basis to write your own:

Today's Date

Letitia Lockheed, Editor
Really Romantic Publishers
123 Lovebird Lane
Harmony, USA

Dear Letitia Lockheed:

I have read most of the romance novels published by your company over the years and think very highly of them. I would like to offer my services to your company as a researcher for the writers of these novels.

My background includes working as a research assistant for Professor Wheatly at Anytown Community College. I tutor students at Anytown High School in history and I am an active member of the Society for Creative Anachronism. I have a special interest in the history of England and France.

I would be happy to come in for an interview at your convenience. Please contact me at the address and phone number listed below. Thank you for your consideration.

Sincerely,

(signature)

Rebecca Researcher
123 Main St.
Anytown, USA
123-4567

Working for Independent Authors

As an independent researcher, you can also work for independent authors who have not yet sold their work to a big publishing house. How do you find these authors? Attend writer's conferences, book fairs, book signings, and seminars. Don't just stand there — as the saying goes, "press the flesh." In other words, introduce yourself, shake hands, and strike up a conversation. This is your big chance to meet the authors in person — so meet as many as you can! See the list of writer's conferences in the back of this book for the ones nearest you. You can find even more listings in the *Literary Market Place*.

A special note: if you have an insider's knowledge in a particular nonfiction area — whether it's medicine or legal matters or how to raise tropical birds — check the *Literary Market Place* or *Writer's Market* for specialty publishers or specific editors at the larger publishing houses to contact.

Don't let the need for a little work up front stop you. There is no better way to begin your job as a researcher than to find out exactly which publishers and writers might need your help!

So jump right in and don't give up for one second until you find the contacts you need to succeed. Let the example of *The Book of Virtues* at the beginning of this chapter inspire you to new heights of success in this fascinating field!

Chapter 11: Reading Movie Scripts and Plays for Profit

Did you know that it's possible to get paid for reading plays and screenplays? Well, it's true. Not only is it possible, but readers are a vital part of the movie and theater business!

It helps if you live in or near New York City, Los Angeles, Washington, D.C., Chicago, or another major metropolitan area. Big cities are where most of the producers and production companies, studios, and literary agents are located. In Los Angeles alone, it's estimated that over 100,000 screenplays are submitted every year. Somebody has to read and evaluate them, and you can bet that the studio and theater executives aren't the people who do that. This market is wide open for readers just like you!

But even though the entertainment industry is centered in New York and Los Angeles, rest assured there are opportunities in this very profitable business in many other parts of the country as well. More and more, movies are being made in states like the Carolinas and Texas, where costs are low and movies can stay within their budgets. Smaller cities and towns are bursting with resident theaters and outposts of the big movie production companies. Famous directors, actors, and producers often make their homes outside of New York and Los Angeles. You can get to know these people and the staff who surround them — and once they know you, you can get your foot in the door!

How It Works

Most often movie scripts (known as "screenplays") and theater scripts are given to readers to evaluate. With thousands of unsolicited screenplays and plays coming over the transom, the only way producers and directors can deal with them is to hand them over to readers like you.

Your challenge as a reader is to sort through these piles of manuscripts and discover the diamond in the rough. But even the lumps of coal need written evaluations. In the industry, these evaluations are known as "coverage." You submit your coverage to the producer or agent who requests it in written form, using a standard format like the one you'll find at the end of this chapter.

Generally speaking, in terms of screenplays, the fee paid to a freelance reader is between $50 and $75 per script. Once you've proven yourself as a good freelance reader, you can send examples of your coverage to larger production companies to get more work and more money.

The Pot of Gold: The Reader's Union

The goal of a serious freelance reader is to become a member of the Reader's Union. Once you're in the union, it will be that much easier for you to find work at one of the big studios or production companies.

The way to become a union member is to do lots of script evaluations for a production company that's large enough to sponsor you and likes you enough to bring you into the union. (They have to like you, because it costs them money to bring you in!)

Here's the great news: the pay scale minimum for a union member is around $33,000 a year! The job requires that you read and write coverage for eight scripts a week. Now, that's not a lot of scripts to read for that kind of money! Could this be your dream job? Here's what a professional reader has to say:

Notes from A Professional Reader

The movie script reader we interviewed for this book was quick to say that she found the job demanding, but she was pleased to be paid so well and be able to work from her home. She began as a freelance reader, and used that as a basis for finally landing a job as a professional script reader for Disney Studios where she worked for five years. She currently works for Fox.

The worst part of her job, she says, is reading the endless supply of really bad scripts. Occasionally she finds a good one, recommends it, and most often that script gets made into a movie. According to her, really good scripts are so rare that just about every one of them ends up being produced!

This reader says that what makes a script stand out for her, and what the top executives are looking for, is the following:

- Strong visual scenes

- Interesting characters

- Good dialogue

- A fresh take on an old story

How to Break In

Go on a search in your geographic area for outposts of the entertainment industry. Start with your phone book and then enlist the help of your reference librarian. Get names and phone numbers of local production companies. Don't assume that there aren't any. Even the smallest towns can provide a retreat for rich and famous people from the film industry. Talk to everyone you know. You can even keep your ears open for name-dropping in the local coffee shop!

For example, I used to live in a small town in Arizona. That's the last place you'd expect to find anyone from the film industry, right? Wrong! Simply by running an ad in the local paper for my home typing service, I got a call from a well-known science fiction writer who needed his manuscripts typed. Several of his books had been made into movies. He was holing up in our small town to get away from the pressures of Hollywood. Lots of other people do the same thing. Who knows, you might find out that a famous movie producer lives within 100 miles of your door!

Once you find a production company near you, you have nothing to lose by calling a staff person and asking if they need to have script submissions read and evaluated. Before you're hired, you'll probably be asked to submit a critique that you wrote. Ask them if you can try yourself out on one of the scripts they have lying around. By all means, try your hand at writing critiques before you call, using the format you'll find at the end of this chapter. Another good idea is to educate yourself by taking classes in screenwriting at your local community college.

You can also educate yourself by mail order. One of the best sources for learning about screenwriting is Truby's Writers Studio. You can call toll-free at 1-800-33-TRUBY to get a copy of their catalog. They offer a full line of audiotapes, videotapes, and computer programs that will teach you everything there is to know about screenwriting — and with that kind of knowledge, you'll be all set to write great coverage!

Reading Plays for Pay

Reading plays is very similar to reading screenplays. The primary difference is that the theater makes slightly different demands on a script. For instance, theatrical pieces are much more dependent on sparkling dialogue and interesting characters who express their inner thoughts. Otherwise, the questions you should ask about a play are the same as the ones that apply to a screenplay.

Most theaters have artistic directors. Some resident theater groups also have literary managers, but many do not. Often it falls to the artistic director, or managing director, to read all new script submissions—a job they are only too happy to pass on to someone like you! Although the pay is not a princely sum, some theaters can afford to compensate a reader at $25 to $50 per script and evaluation. Find out who the artistic director is at your local theater and call or write to inquire if there is a need for your services.

You'll need to establish yourself as someone who's serious about the theater in order to break in. But if you go to lots of plays, read lots of plays, and practice writing coverage according to the guidelines in this chapter, you'll be more than up to the task!

When reading for a theater, be sure to ask the artistic director exactly what he wants to know about the script. You should also be clear as to the format he would prefer for your evaluation. You may not need to use a format as extensive as the one at the end of this chapter. In any case, start out with a "log line" that summarizes the basic story in not more than two or three sentences.

When you don't like a play, most theaters are satisfied with a paragraph or two describing what you feel doesn't work about it, with some substantiating comments. When a play is interesting to you, a much more thorough description as to why it works, what the characters are like, examples of good dialogue, etc. should be included in your evaluation.

After carefully studying Chapter 18, "How to Read Critically," and using the guidelines for writing coverage in this chapter, go for it!

How to Evaluate Scripts and Plays

The first step in writing coverage is to attentively read the script or play. The objective is to let yourself be drawn into the story even as you're noticing why that is happening to you. Or conversely, if you're not being drawn in, to note why that's not happening. Ask yourself the following questions:

- Is there a clear protagonist? Or, if it's a script about an ensemble of characters, are they arranged well around a common goal, and/or theme?

- Is the goal of the protagonist(s) visible, desirable and achievable? Even if you wouldn't want what they want, can you see why they would want it?

- Is the conflict clearly drawn?

- Does it get harder and harder for the protagonist to achieve his goal?

- Is there something that the protagonist is missing (physically and/or emotionally) that because of the journey he or she is on, will help them to learn something, i.e. to become more loving, or more trusting?

- Is the antagonist a real threat to the hero? Is the antagonist as smart as the hero, as powerful or more powerful than the hero, so that the hero is truly challenged?

- What is the theme of the script? (See Chapter 3 of this book for a discussion of what a theme is.)

- What is the premise? (This is the thought behind the story. See Chapter 3 for a discussion of what a premise is.)

- Is there a distinctive feeling in the script for time and place?

- Is the script visual? Especially in a screenplay, what are the big scenes, the set pieces that make the script worth filming? In a musical stage play, the same questions apply. Even plays should be visually interesting. (On the evaluation form, this is what is called "Cinematic/Production Values.")

- Is this a good concept for a movie or a play? (For instance, the concept of "Free Willy" was "young boy frees trapped orca." The concept of "Tootsie" was "an out-of-work actor dresses like a woman in order to get an acting job.")

Is the concept interesting in terms of the protagonist and the specific journey they are on? Do you care? If so, why? If you don't care, why not? Have we seen this before? If so, is it a fresh take on an old concept?

Writing the Coverage

This is exactly what it sounds like. Your written evaluation will cover, or report on, the script. The purpose of the coverage is to give the producer, director, or agent, a clear idea what the script is about, and also to state the strength and weaknesses of plot, character, dialogue, and concept. Based on these criteria, you then say whether or not (in your opinion) the script would be suitable for staging or filming.

Unless the producer specifically gives you a form to fill out, copy the format from the example provided in this chapter. Fill in the title, author, the date you read the piece, the genre, the locale of the screenplay (where the action takes place), circa (time period), draft date (the one the writer has put on the script), length (number of pages), and your name where it says "analyst."

The following are the categories to be addressed in the order they should appear in your coverage.

The Log Line:

Think of this as a *TV GUIDE* blurb summarizing the script. Usually two sentences.

The Comment Summary:

This is probably best written last, after you've written your full comments. Generally it should only be three or four sentences long. (See example below)

Directly beneath this the ratings table should appear. This is where you grade the listed categories by placing an X under EXCELLENT, GOOD, FAIR, POOR. Next you should have a place to mark your overall evaluation, both for the writer of the script, and for your recommendation for the project. These categories are listed below in the example.

The Synopsis:

This should be no more than two pages, double-spaced. Eliminate unnecessary secondary characters. Think of the synopsis as your chance to turn the script into a little story. In other words, as best as possible, write it so that it flows easily and makes sense.

The Comments:

The first paragraph is an overall impression of the script. In the first sentence of this first paragraph, include a brief description of the concept.

The second paragraph is a two to three sentence summary of the plot. We have to presume that the executive doesn't read the script, but rather only looks at the log line and the comments.

The third, fourth and fifth paragraphs break down your reasons for liking (or not liking) the script. Did the writer have a good concept (i.e., is it fresh, interesting, even a new take on an old concept)? If not, why do you think it didn't work (i.e., is the concept unworkable, or tired, or boring)? Did the writer have a good idea, but then didn't properly see it through (i.e., the plot went in the wrong direction)?

This is where most writers fail — they have a decent idea but don't know what to do with it to maximize potential. Often, they don't establish the set-up quickly enough, so that we're confused as to where the story is headed. Another problem could be that we simply don't like the protagonist's goal.

Also, think about the script's structure. Is there a clear act break somewhere between pages 25 and 40? Is there another act break around page 90? At the end of the second act (usually around page 90), do we see the protagonist at his lowest ebb?

Divide your paragraphs into clear, concise thoughts. If, for example, you talk about the protagonist's goal being poor, make that a separate paragraph.

Then make your next thought another paragraph. Remember, it's easier to read a page that has lots of white space. Long paragraphs with numerous thoughts are difficult to get through. Think of your evaluation as a newspaper article with short, easy-to-read paragraphs.

Always support your comments. Whenever you're trying to make a point, cite specific examples from the script. This makes it easy for the executive to call an agent and pretend that he's read the script.

If the script reminds you of a film, particularly a recent one, be sure to mention it.

When you get to your sixth paragraph, you should comment on the protagonist's relationships to the key supporting characters. Here is where you mention whether or not the antagonist was a good foil for the hero.

The seventh paragraph briefly covers dialogue, pacing, and structure.

The eighth paragraph concludes your comments and summarizes your feelings again. Try not to say exactly the same thing you did in the first paragraph.

Finally, if at all possible, try to emulate this format. Below you'll find an example of actual script coverage written according to the format.

Chapter 11: Reading Movie Scripts and Plays for Profit 133

SAMPLE COVERAGE

TITLE: BOND VOYAGE   DATE: XX/XX/XX

AUTHOR: XXX XXXX   GENRE: Comedy Adventure

SUBMITTED TO: XXX Productions   LOCALE: U.S. suburb & ocean

SUBMITTED BY: The Authors   CIRCA: Present day

ANALYST: XXX XXXX

DRAFT DATE: 1994

FORM/LENGTH: Screenplay; 111 pp

LOGLINE: A young man, who believes himself to be James Bond, battles a serial killer at sea.

COMMENT SUMMARY: This ill-conceived comic adventure allegedly satirizes the James Bond genre, but it is neither humorous nor faithful to the 007 formula. The tone is ugly, with brutal violence, the protagonist is unsympathetic, and the story doesn't build to a strong conclusion.

	EXCELLENT	GOOD	FAIR	POOR
Premise/Concept			X	X
Plot/Structure				X
Characterization			X	
Dialogue				X
Cinematic/Prod. Values			X	X

WRITER EVALUATION   RECOMMEND:____   CONSIDER:____   PASS: _X__

PROJECT EVALUATION   RECOMMEND:____   CONSIDER:____   PASS: _X__

SYNOPSIS: Handsome JIM WRIGHT has longed to be James Bond since he was a small boy—he would spend his days pretending to be the famed secret agent. Subsequently, by the time Jim becomes an adult, he has grown into a very noble but confused man—he genuinely believes that he is James Bond.

Meanwhile, IVAN TRELLIBOSKIN has always been a sociopath. As a child, he tormented his parents, and as an adult, he has become a serial killer. Managing to escape a prison hospital, Ivan decides that his next victim will be Jim (because they share the same psychiatrist).

SAMPLE COVERAGE

While vacationing at sea, Jim wins the attentions of many young women, who are drawn to his good looks and charm. However, when one of Jim's lovers turns up dead, the young man is questioned for murder by the ship's CAPTAIN. When two more people Jim knows also turn up dead, he is placed in the brig.

Jim is freed by a CIA agent, OPHELIA PORK, who explains that she knows Jim is innocent and that the real killer is Ivan, who has stowed away on board the ship. With Ophelia working at his side, Jim attempts to locate Ivan, but instead Ivan finds him—the crafty killer has murdered the Captain and secretly taken his place. After holding a mock trial, Ivan throws Jim overboard with some chum (made from Ophelia's body), hoping that sharks will eat the young man.

Jim manages to elude the sharks and swims to a nearby island, where he rescues a beautiful woman, LILITH, who has been abducted by natives. Stealing a boat, they return to the U.S.

Knowing that Ivan will hunt him down, Jim hides Lilith (with whom he has fallen in love), then waits for the killer to appear. Sure enough, Jim receives a visit from AMANDA, a beautiful call girl hired by Ivan. When Amanda lures Jim to bed, Ivan throws a trigger and the bed is impaled by sharp spikes. Amanda is killed, but Jim escapes unharmed to confront Ivan. After a brief fight, Jim allows Ivan to fall from a window to his death. As the story ends, Jim reunites with Lilith, and for the first time in his life, assumes his true identity. His days as James Bond are over.

COMMENTS: It is difficult to say what the point of this screenplay is. Although this is ostensibly a comic adventure satirizing the James Bond genre, the tone is too dark, the violence is explicit and the story has nothing to do with any Bond story. Clearly, the authors have only a concept (what if a man thought he was James Bond) and don't understand the genre they're writing about.

The plot finds Jim, a man who believes himself to be James Bond, vacationing at sea. There, he is framed for numerous murders by a serial killer, Ivan, who is stalking him.

The problem with this script is basic: there is no reason for the writers to use the James Bond element. The story is nothing like a 007 adventure—Bond has never confronted a serial killer—and therefore, the script does not qualify as satire. Indeed, this work is so extremely violent (one woman is burned to death, another impaled on spikes) that it undercuts what little humor the story manages to achieve.

SAMPLE COVERAGE

The story doesn't succeed as adventure, either. This is not an intricate plot—a serial killer stalks Jim—and is exploitative! Whenever the plot lags (which is often), the writers kill another person.

Throughout, the writers make mistakes. Rather than being the pursuer (which is what you'd expect the protagonist to be), Jim is a victim who is constantly framed for murder. There is no progression to the story—the writers simply introduce a love interest, and then kill her. Jim doesn't have a goal—he is reactionary, not active. The villain, Ivan, has a goal that is nebulous at best (he wants to kill Jim because they share the same psychiatrist).

It should also be noted that it's difficult to identify with a protagonist who is delusional and fantasizing about a character most people outgrow at a young age. This quirk in Jim's character makes him very childlike... and not the least bit like the secret agent.

The script's tone is decidedly ugly as the writers aren't content with simply killing characters—they have to be mutilated, as well. Particularly reprehensible—Ophelia, a seemingly important supporting character, is cut into small pieces and then thrown into shark-infested waters.

These flaws clearly illustrate the writers don't have a handle on their script. If this is a satire of the James Bond genre, why isn't the protagonist caught up in a larger-than-life adventure, and why is the violence so explicit?

To conclude, there is no reason to pursue this project. The protagonist is unsympathetic and his "adventure" exploitative.

PASS ON SCRIPT

PASS ON WRITERS

136 Chapter 11: Reading Movie Scripts and Plays for Profit

Chapter 12:
The Audiobook Market

A huge industry was born in 1983 when one of America's leading booksellers, Waldenbooks, cleared off some prime shelf space and stocked a new product called "audiobooks." These recordings of books on cassette tapes proved to be a big hit. Before long other major book chains followed suit, and the rest, as they say, is history.

Today audiobooks are everywhere. They aren't just for old people or for blind people — far from it! People listen to audiobooks in their cars while commuting to and from work, or around the house while they're doing chores, or while they're pursuing hobbies from stamp collecting to knitting. Teenagers listen to audiobooks with their Walkmans on as they rollerblade or hang out in the park. Kids love audiobooks, too — they can read along while hearing the words spoken by a friendly voice, a big selling point for busy moms and dads who aren't always available to read books aloud the old-fashioned way.

To find out just how big the audiobook market is, you might want to take a look at Words on Cassette, which is a directory similar to Books in Print for the audiobook market. Ask for it at your local library. This publication lists over 1,000 publishers of spoken word audio tapes. Not only that, but there are now over 100 bookstores around the country that carry nothing but audiobooks!

According to an industry spokesperson at the Audio Publishing Association, spoken word audio sales accounted for a record $1.3 billion retail market in 1994, which represented a 40% growth increase from 1993. This is obviously a hot and fast-growing field—and if you have the basic skills to qualify, it's a field loaded with opportunities for readers like you!

Finding a Niche as an Audio Book Reader

Although there is obviously quite a bit of work available for voice talent on all of these audiobooks now flooding the bookstores, first we must offer you a word of caution. This is an almost "invisible" job market. Some audiobook publishers are almost secretive about their hiring practices because they don't want to be besieged by unsolicited sample tapes sent in the mail or by phone calls from people they don't know who are looking for work.

The top readers in the field are professional actors and actresses with a drama background. Many of these readers are represented by agents who contact the audio publishing firms on their behalf. Some audiobook publishers will only hire members of AFTRA (American Federation of Television and Recording Artists), a professional union. The biggest audiobook publishers, for example, Random House, use only celebrity readers — famous authors, actors, and actresses. There are about 150 major audiobook publishers in the country who rely on professional talent like this.

But does that mean there's a shortage of opportunities for people like you? Far from it! Medium-sized audiobook publishing companies generally keep a house talent pool of 40–50 voices that they call upon to record new titles. Be advised that turnover is low, as people tend to hold on to these plum jobs. This kind of work is usually part-time since a voice, even a good one, can only last so long in a studio reading a book. But if you're a housewife or working person with a great reading voice, the part-time nature of this kind of work will probably suit you to a T!

If you've got what it takes, you owe it to yourself to investigate being an audiobook reader. This chapter will walk you through the particulars of how to find work in the brave new world of audiobooks!

What Constitutes a Good Voice?

First and foremost, audiobook companies are looking for good readers. According to one insider in the business, "You either have the knack or you don't." You need good articulation — in other words, you must speak clearly — plus good voice quality. Last, but not least, your voice must sound appealing on tape!

Most books are read straight through by one reader or "voice," who is responsible for portraying all the characters in a book. An exception would be a book that contains chapters by more than one first-person narrator. In that case, several readers might be hired, one for each first-person narrator.

Although some companies ask you to use a neutral voice throughout, most of them want you to use voice characterization, meaning that you give each character a slightly different voice or approach. This doesn't mean that you have to sound like a cartoon, totally changing your voice for each new character. Instead, as the narrative voice, you bring life to the story by slowing it down or speeding it up, adding pathos or excitement, and bringing subtle dimensions and shadings to different characters. If you have the ability, you might add regional dialects or a foreign language.

In short, you must approach the book as an actor would, with an actor's training and skill. This doesn't necessarily mean you must have years of acting classes — though that would certainly help. In fact, any dramatic training you might have will be put to good use in the audiobook trade. But the main thing is your voice must have the power to bring a story to life. You might have a background in commercials, voice-overs, or radio announcing — or, you might just be a natural!

Experience May Not Be Necessary

One voice talent recruiter said that some of her readers approach their first audition never having done this kind of work before, hit it running cold, and lo and behold, it turns out that they have the gift of breathing life into books. She also warned that just because you're good reading to your kids doesn't mean you'd be well suited to this exacting line of work — but then again, you might be.

Just remember, you either have it or you don't — these companies will not train you! Making a story come alive is a skill that probably can't be taught. But if you have it, there are virtually no barriers to your success! We know of a grandmother in the Midwest whose special talent was holding kids absolutely spellbound with her renditions of famous fairy tales. Her son started a series of audiobooks with his mom as the featured reader, and the tapes sold like hotcakes!

The audiobook industry offers awards to recordings that demonstrate exceptional narrative voice, style, and vocal characterizations. Find some of these award-winning tapes and listen to them yourself so you can hear the magic. That's the kind of professionalism you'll be striving for as you make your way in the world of audiobooks!

Practice Your Reading Skills

Maybe you have children at home who you read to all the time, and you get all the practice reading out loud that you need. But if you need practice reading out loud to others, try calling The Braille Institute in your community. Most good-sized cities and towns have a center for The Braille Institute — and they are always in need of volunteers to read to the blind. By volunteering on a regular basis, you can develop your reading skills in ways you never thought possible — plus, you'll be doing something worthwhile for others in the process!

The other great thing you can do to become an expert reader is get involved in your local theater community. Take acting classes and participate in theater productions. Work backstage, be an usher, or try out for some of the smaller roles. You don't have to be the star of the show; just about anything you do in the theater is bound to help improve your reading abilities, simply because you're exposing yourself to how it's done!

Getting in the Door

Forget about the biggest companies — the publishing giants who have the financial resources to hire big name actors, authors, and celebrities.

Instead, target mid-sized firms. We interviewed some well respected, mid-sized firms from around the country who specialize in audiobooks to obtain some inside tips to help you break in.

As we said earlier, some companies, especially those located in big cities with easy access to theatrical talent, generally hire professional union actors through agents. Of all the companies we talked to, though, most said they welcomed new talent to try their luck and that audition processes were ongoing. In fact most of the companies said they were always interested in hiring the right new talent for their reader's pool.

A good place to start is the list of audiobook publishers printed at the end of this chapter. Look to see if any of them are located in your area. Most companies will not hire anyone who lives outside their immediate vicinity. Most companies are also unwilling to take unsolicited phone calls and sample tapes of your voice, too. Like we said before, it's a challenge to break in, but don't get discouraged! The best route is to write a letter or get to know someone who will introduce you to the publisher as a good candidate. A sample letter is included at the end of this chapter.

If you're lucky, the publisher will ask you to come in for an audition or to submit a home recording done on "any old equipment." You'll probably be asked to select and read five minutes of a modern novel for which you feel well-cast. If you go for an audition in person, you can expect to go into a recording studio where you'll read for a brief amount of time. Then the publisher will play back the recording to see how you sound on tape. If they like your voice, you're in!

We can't emphasize enough that this is an "insider's" job market that you must cultivate with care. Word of mouth works best in this industry. You may find some insider contacts right under your nose! The best place to start is your local theater community. For example, one audiobook company we talked to works with a drama professor at a nearby university who does readings himself and also recommends students and people from the community as readers. Now, that's just the kind of person you want to get to know. If you're not already involved in your local theater community, now's the time to start!

If there's an audiobook publishing company near you, chances are they already have an established relationship with the local theater community. Ask around. When you find a reader who works for the company you're interested in, ask them if the company is hiring and what approach to use to break in. Of course, if the reader you've met likes you, they may decide to recommend you directly to the publisher — this is the best-case scenario!

Working Conditions

Most readers are independent contractors working part-time on a project-by-project basis. Some publishing firms have their own in-house recording studios, while others contract out to commercial recording studios.

When it's time to do the recording, you'll go straight to the recording studio with a studio manager who acts as the director. If you make a mistake, it's corrected on the spot; you go back to exactly where you make an error, correct it and keep on reading. When you're finished reading the book, the master tape is completed and duplicated for commercial distribution.

Some readers receive a flat hourly fee while others receive a royalty on every tape sold. When you first start out, you can expect to get an hourly rate of about $20 per hour. Once you're more established, and as you get more familiar with the industry, you may be able to negotiate a royalty agreement. That means you get ongoing income for reading a single book — an arrangement that will keep you smiling all the way to the bank! Every royalty agreement is different, but the usual range is 5% to 10% of the retail price of each cassette that's sold. See even more information about potential earnings at the end of this chapter!

Get to Know Publications About Audiobooks

Pay a visit to the reference desk at your local library and ask for Recorded Books, Inc. This publication is about 170 pages long and comes out four times a year. It lists new recorded books, and it's well worth your time and effort to become familiar with the field. Books on Tape, which comes out once a year, gives complete audiobook listings as well.

Your reference librarian probably has boxes of catalogues from audiobook companies lying around. Ask if you can look at these periodicals and catalogs. Even though they are designed for librarians, they can give you valuable information about audiobook companies. Among other things, you'll learn the kinds of titles they record and how many titles they publish each year. You'll also pick up some names of contacts at specific companies. Make copies of this information or write it down — then follow up on the companies in your area that interest you.

Another great source of information on audiobooks is a monthly magazine called Audiofile. Again, your librarian may have a copy of this magazine that you can borrow. Check it out for advertisements and reviews of new audiobooks. By doing research in this way, you'll discover the names of possible contacts and be that much closer to finding work as a reader.

For a mere $6.95, you can send for Audiofile's Audiobook Reference Guide. This guide has an extensive list of audiobook publishers and distributors. To order, call 207/774-7563.

Get Hooked Yourself!

It goes without saying that if you want to break into this field as a reader, you need to know the product! Become a regular listener yourself. Your local library probably has a great selection of audiobooks that you can check out for free. Then there's Waldenbooks and all the other big bookstore chains, where you can find audiobooks on virtually every subject under the sun.

As you listen to more and more audiobooks, you'll discover a phenomenon that is familiar to fans of this art form: by the time you've finished listening to the tape of an entire book, the reader has become your friend! And if you like that particular reader, you'll automatically want to seek out other books narrated by the same person! Some readers, like Flo Gibson of the Classic Books on Cassettes Collection, have recorded hundreds of books and have won awards from numerous publishing and audio organizations. She gets fan letters from people all over the country, and the world!

That's the wonderful thing about being a reader for audiobooks. Even if you're not famous already, you have the potential to become a celebrity in your own right. People from all walks of life will seek out your voice as a favorite companion as they listen to their favorite audiobooks. Plus, you'll be making money doing something you love — a combination that can't be beat!

AFTRA: Join the Union!

As you get more established in the audiobook industry, you might want to consider joining AFTRA, which stands for American Federation of TV and Radio Artists. There are no special membership requirements to join this union; anyone can join. The catch is, you have to come up with the one-time membership fee: $800. After that, it only costs you $42.50 a year

Sample Letter to Audiobook Publishers

Today's Date

Jane Doe, Production Manager
ABC Audiobooks
123 Main Street
Anytown, USA 45678

Dear Jane:

I am writing to inquire about opportunities for becoming an audiobook reader at your company. I have a BA in Drama from Anytown Community College and have appeared in many local productions, most recently as Juliet in Anytown Theater's critically acclaimed production of Romeo and Juliet.

A review of that production is enclosed. My other experience includes reading radio plays on Anytown Community College's radio station, KXYZ FM.

Please let me know if I could come in for an audition at your convenience. You can reach me at 333-4444.

Thank you for your consideration, and I look forward to hearing from you.

Sincerely,

(signature)

Roberta Reader
333 Media St.
Anytown, USA 21000

to maintain your membership. What you get for your membership is a BIG pay increase: $85 to $200 per hour! You must be a true professional, however, to command these rates. Keep this opportunity in mind as you pursue your career as an audiobook reader—with all the experience you'll soon be getting, it won't take you long to achieve that goal!

For more information, contact AFTRA at 212/532-0800 (New York City) or 213/461-8111 (Los Angeles).

Audiobook Publishers

There are over 1,000 publishers and distributors of audiobooks nationwide. This list gives you just a small sample. For a complete list, consult Words on Cassette, a reference book that you can find at your local library.

Keep in mind that audiobook publishers can only use readers who live close enough to their offices to come in for an audition. Do not waste your time and theirs if you live too far away! If you don't find an audiobook publisher near you on this list, don't be discouraged. Just hightail it for your local library and consult the reference book we talked about earlier in this chapter, Words on Cassette — with over 1,000 audiobook publishers in this country, there's bound to be one near you!

Read this chapter thoroughly before you write these companies and follow the format of the sample letter carefully, including any relevant experience you might have. Good luck and happy reading!

American Audio Literature
(Fiction, Children's, Suspense, Western, Mystery, Science Fiction)
PO Box 1392
Cicero, NY 13039

American Audio Prose Library
(Fiction, Nonfiction, Mystery, Science Fiction, Short Story, Biography, Humor, Poetry, Interviews)
PO Box 842
Columbia, MO 65205

Artana Productions
(Fiction, Children's, Storytelling)
PO Box 1054
Marshfield, MA 02050

Audio Bookshelf
(Fiction, Nonfiction, Classics, Story Collections, Children's, Serious Fiction)
RR1, Box 706
Belfast, ME 04915

Audio Entertainment
(Fiction)
PO Box 461059
Aurora, CO 80046

Audio Literature
(Fiction, Nonfiction, Best Sellers, Serious Fiction, Parenting, Humor, Religion, Short Stories, Classics, Biography, History, Personal Development)
3800 Palos Verdes Way
South San Francisco, CA 94080

Audio Renaissance Tapes
(Fiction, Nonfiction, Children's, Serious Fiction, Biography, History, Business, How-to, Humor, Story Collections, Classics, Best Sellers, Suspense, Mystery, Science Fiction, Personal Development)
5858 Wilshire Blvd., Suite 205
Los Angeles, CA 90036

August House
(Children's, Storytelling, Parenting, Humor)
PO Box 3223
Little Rock, AR 72203

Blackstone Audio Books
(Fiction, Nonfiction, Children's, Best Sellers, Western, Mystery, Science Fiction, Biography)
PO Box 969
Ashland, OR 97520

Books in Motion
(Fiction, Nonfiction, Children's, Science Fiction, Suspense, Western, Business, Best Sellers)
East 9212 Montgomery, Suite 501
Spokane, WA 99206

Brilliance Corporation
(Fiction, Nonfiction, Business, Serious Fiction, Classics, Suspense, Western, Mystery, Best Sellers, Science Fiction)
PO Box 887
Grand Haven, MI 49417

Buckingham Classics
(Fiction, Nonfiction, Children's, Story Collections, Classics, Suspense, Western, Mystery, Science Fiction, Horror, History, How-to, Humor)
1240 West Arthur
Chicago, IL 60626

Dartnell Corporation
(Business, Personal Development)
4660 N. Ravenswood Ave.
Chicago, IL 60640

Dercum Audio
(Fiction, Children's, Best Sellers, Science Fiction, Story Collections, Classics, Mystery, Horror, Fantasy)
PO Box 1425
West Chester, PA 19380

Dual Dolphin Publishing, Inc.
(Fiction, Nonfiction, Children's, Biography, Suspense, Mystery, History, Travel, Humor, Religion, Serious Fiction, Story Collections, Classics)
475 Washington
Wrentham, MA 02093

Durkin Hayes
(Fiction, Nonfiction, Children's, Best Sellers, Story Collections, Classics, Suspense, Westerns, Mystery, Science Fiction, Horror, Biography, Humor)
1 Colomba Dr.
Niagara Falls, NY 12430

Earwig Music Co.
(Children's, Storytelling, Horror)
1818 W. Pratt Blvd.
Chicago, IL 60626

Educational Excursions
(Nonfiction, Biography, History, Travel)
PO Box 180355
Dallas, TX 75218

Folktellers
(Children's, Storytelling, Humor)
PO Box 2898
Asheville, NC 28802

Green Island Productions, Inc.
(Fiction, Nonfiction, Classics, Serious Fiction, Biography, History, Business, Personal Development, Religion)
PO Box 368
324 Wells St.
Greenfield, MA 01302

High Windy Audio
(Children's, Parenting, Storytelling)
PO Box 553
Fairview, NC 28730

Highbridge Audio
(Fiction, Nonfiction, Best Sellers, Serious Fiction, Horror, Biography, History, Business, Humor, Story Collections, Classics, Suspense, Science Fiction, Personal Development, Parenting, Religion)
1000 Westgate Dr.
St. Paul, MN 55114

Knowledge Products
(Nonfiction, Classics, History, Science, Religion)
PO Box 305151
Nashville, TN 37230

Listening Library
(Fiction, Children's, Story Collections, Classics, Suspense, Mystery, Science Fiction, Humor)
1 Park Ave.
Old Greenwich, CT 06870

The Mind's Eye
(Fiction, Nonfiction, Children's, Story Collections, Classics, Mystery, Horror, Humor, Westerns)
4 Commercial Blvd.
Novato, CA 94949

National Storytelling Press
(Classics, Suspense, Westerns, Storytelling, History, Parenting, Humor, Religion, Mystery)
PO Box 309
216 Headtown Rd.
Jonesborough, TN 37659

Northword Audio Press
(Nonfiction, Story Collections, Natural History, Nature)
PO Box 1360
Minocqua, WI 54540

Parabola Audio Library
(Nonfiction, Children's, Personal Development, Biography)
656 Broadway, Suite 615
New York, NY 10012

Peachtree Publishers
(Fiction, Children's, Storytelling)
494 Armour Circle NE
Atlanta, GA 30324

The Publishing Mills
(Fiction, Nonfiction, Children's, Serious Fiction, Mystery, Science Fiction, Biography, History, Best Sellers, Story Collections, Classics, Suspense, Western, Personal Development, Humor)
1680 N. Vine St., Suite 1016
Los Angeles, CA 90028

Rabbit Ears Productions
(Children's, Storytelling)
131 Rowayton Ave.
Rowayton, CT 06853

Recorded Books, Inc.
(Fiction, Nonfiction, Children's, Young Adult, Science Fiction, Horror, Biography, History, Serious Fiction, Best Sellers, Story Collections, Classics, Suspense, Mystery, Business, Language, Travel, Humor, Science, Religion)
270 Skipjack Rd.
Prince Frederick, MD 20678

Ride With Me
(Nonfiction, History, Travel)
PO Box 1324
Bethesda, MD 20817

Rivertree Productions
(Fiction, Children's, Story Collections, Classics, Storytelling)
PO Box 410
Bradford, NH 03221

Sound Horizons
(Nonfiction, Best Sellers, Classics, Religion, Personal Development)
250 W. 57th St., Suite 1527
New York, NY 10107

Sounds True Recording
(Personal Development, Religion)
735 Walnut St.
Boulder, CO 80302

The Spencer Library
(Fiction)
116-200 Village Blvd.
Princeton, NJ 08540

Sunset Productions
(Fiction, Nonfiction, Children's,
Serious Fiction, Western, Mystery,
Science Fiction, Horror, Best Sellers,
Story Collections, Classics, Suspense,
History, Humor, Religion)
369 Montezuma #416
Santa Fe, NM 87501

Weston Woods
(Fiction, Children's, Best Sellers,
Classics, Biography, History,
Storytelling)
389 Newton Turnpike
Weston, CT 06883

Yellow Moon Press
(Storytelling)
PO Box 381316
Cambridge, MA 02238

Chapter 13: Get Your Own Writing Published!

If you love reading books, chances are you've given some thought to writing one of your own. You may even have manuscripts stashed away that are just waiting to be sent out into the world. But how to go about it? That's what this chapter is about.

You may think the odds are stacked against you, and that people who do get published are just plain lucky. But getting your own writing published requires more than luck. Just like baking a cake, certain key ingredients must be present in order for the end result to be a delicious success. By assembling these ingredients beforehand, you vastly improve your chances!

Your first goal is to make a publisher, editor, agent, or theater director want to read your manuscript at all. Once the person with the power is convinced you are a serious writer, the next challenge is to make that person respond to what is on the page — to make them want to keep turning the pages. This chapter will show you how to present your writing, how to make your writing worthy of reading, and how to market your manuscript.

Keys to a Professional Presentation

Part of the success of any venture is looking good going in — like getting dressed up for a job interview, or wrapping a present in beautiful paper. Today more than ever before, you need a professional presentation in order to submit your manuscript to a publisher. Because the volume of submissions is so high, and because most editors have a very limited amount of time, it is only the professional-looking manuscripts that receive any attention at all.

Use these guidelines to make your manuscript stand out in the crowd!

1. Show That You're Serious

Always use the best cotton bond paper you can afford for printing out final copies of your manuscripts. If all you have available is a typewriter, find one with a self-correcting feature, and always use a new jet-black ribbon. Use a computer to type your manuscripts if at all possible. The quality of the printer your computer uses is very important. Never, ever, under penalty of constant rejection, use a dot matrix printer to print out your manuscripts for submission to a publisher. If you don't have a laser printer, save all your money to buy one. In the meantime, take your computer disk to a store that has laser printers, like Kinko's Copy Shops, and have them print out your manuscript for you.

2. Show That You Know the Genre

This is as simple as knowing the acceptable typed format for a play, or knowing that newspaper articles always have the symbol "###" or "-30-" at the end, or that novels are broken down into chapters. Most editors will not give a manuscript a chance, let alone a second glance, if it appears that the writer hasn't bothered to read and learn about proper format, including margins and spacing. Every library has books that will show you exactly how to arrange the words on the page according to the type of writing you are submitting.

One of the best guides is *The Writer's Digest Guide to Manuscript Formats*, by Dian Dincin Buchman and Seli Groves, published by Writer's Digest Books. You can order this book by calling toll-free, 1-800-289-0963. The price is $19.99, and it's well worth it to make sure your manuscript's format is picture-perfect! All Writer's Digest books come with a 30-day, money-back guarantee. Writer's Digest publishes many other useful books on writing as well; for a complete list, pick up a copy of *Writer's Digest* magazine at your local bookstore!

As a general rule, double space your manuscript and leave margins of at least 1 ½ inches all around. Make sure your spelling and grammar are perfect! (See Chapter 2 for details.)

Stick to the genre. A great many writing submissions are rejected because they can't be easily categorized. New writers frequently try to make their writing fit more than one category — but this is a big mistake! For example, if you're writing a nonfiction article for a magazine about the epidemic of teenage pregnancy in America, resist the temptation to turn it into a novel by telling the full-length version of your own story. It may be appropriate to tell your own story briefly, but another genre would be better suited for that purpose.

Or, if you're writing a short story, don't try to use it as an opportunity to prove your point of view on a political or socially debatable issue. Write a letter to your local newspaper instead. This is good writing practice, and newspapers are practically the only place left for preaching in print.

However, you can have a character in a play or a novel rant and rave and be as opinionated as a radio talk show host, just as long as you have another character who expresses the opposite point of view.

3. Show That You Are Familiar With the Publication

It is absolutely essential that you read the magazines, newspapers, or books that an editor has published before. Reading these other publications first will give you a much better chance of actually being published. You'll get a clear idea of what they're looking for, and a clear understanding of how they want the subject matter presented. You'll also gain an understanding of the editor's ideas and the vision that affects their choice of material. By paying attention to such things as tone, vocabulary level, and length of the average article or book, you'll bypass many of the dreaded rejection slips that authors are always talking about.

When you start investigating different book publishers, by all means, write the ones that you're especially interested in and ask them for a copy of their catalog. That way you'll get to see EXACTLY what they publish. Best of all, these catalogs are FREE! Use the addresses in Volume II, or consult *Writer's Market* or the *Literary Market Place*.

4. Cover Letter/Query Letter

Always accompany any submission with a cover letter briefly introducing yourself and your manuscript. If you can describe what you've written in one or two sentences, and you can make it sound exciting, the editor is much more likely to keep reading, and even be intrigued.

Oftentimes a query letter is the best way to approach an editor. This is an introductory letter which queries, or asks, the editor as to whether he or she has any interest in your book or article. Many publishers require this as the first step before you submit an actual manuscript.

The wonderful thing about query letters is that they cut down on personal rejection (after all, the writing isn't being judged, only the idea), and sending a letter instead of the entire manuscript saves many dollars on postage and copying expenses.

If you're not sure whether to send a query letter first, consult a reference book like *Writer's Market*, which will tell you each publisher's policy about query letters. It's generally a good idea to send a query letter for longer articles or books. It's not usually necessary to send a query letter for an article you're submitting to the local newspaper or for poetry.

Generally speaking, the bigger the publisher and the longer your manuscript, the better off you'll be by sending a query letter before you send the completed manuscript.

Sample Cover Letter

Today's Date

xxx xxx, Editor
Los Angeles Times Magazine
Times Mirror Square
Los Angeles, CA 90053

Dear Mr. XX:

I am inquiring as to your interest in publishing my essay on the "Right to Life" movement. Because I was a member of that organization, I believe your readers might find it enlightening to know what compels an individual to unite themselves with this philosophy and the subsequent thought processes that bring them to a more open-minded view.

I am a professional writer living in Anytown. I am a member of the WGA west and currently write theater criticism for *DramaLogue*.

I can be reached at the address and phone number below.

Sincerely yours,

(signature)

Jane Writer
123 Main Street
Anytown, USA 67890
890-123-4567

Sample Query Letter

Today's Date

xxx xxx
Gospel Publishers
456 Park Ave.
Anytown, USA

Dear xxx:

Thank you for considering me as one of your freelance writers. I've had quite a bit of experience with both children and adults in the context of the church. I have successfully staged a Passion Play, an AIDS play, many family plays, and a Christmas promenade play.

I think the book proposal and sample chapter for *"Hey Kids, Let's Put On A Play!"* speaks for itself. Although intended to be a book for everyone, I think you can see how it could be a great teaching aid for any Sunday School teacher. I hope this sample conveys how much delight I take in doing this kind of writing and the pleasure it gives me to think of new ways to teach and to delight. I have amazing energy for exciting children of all ages and hope that you can see where my talent could be of use to you.

Thanks for your time and consideration. I look forward to hearing from you soon.

Sincerely,

(signature)

Jane Writer
123 Main Street
Anytown, USA 67890
890-123-4567

Essential Ingredients of Good Writing

There are many different ways to become a published writer. Creative writing, such as informative articles, short fiction, novels, plays, book reviews, essays, poetry, theater reviews, and informative columns in newspapers are available to anyone who has something to say.

However, the writing has to be good. But what makes writing good? What makes you want to keep reading someone else's story? What is it about a movie or a play review that compels you to go to the theater, or to stay away? Whatever the type of writing, there are always special elements that make it memorable and compelling. Some of these elements are described below.

1. Desire to Communicate

One need only look at the masters like Shakespeare and Dickens to realize that great works of art communicate well—and continue to do so down through the centuries. That has to be the ultimate reason for writing in the first place—a desire to share what you know and what you feel with someone else, and to make a lasting difference in the world. If you are dedicated and can tell your ego to take a hike while you're writing, you may even enlighten a soul or two, or teach something to someone whose life is improved by a new skill or insight. Or, wonder of wonders, your writing may be so honest and vulnerable that you bring a moment of transcendence to your own life as well as the lives of others.

2. Perception & Originality

Everyone is different. No two people could ever write the same song or paint the same picture, and given identical subject matter, no two people will ever write the same story.

I learned this from Mr. Rogers while making meat loaf one evening for my family. "You are special, you're the only one of your kind," he said.

I was about thirty years old at the time, and up to that point I was not convinced of my own uniqueness. This had probably a lot to do with living in a look-alike house in suburbia with 2.5 children, a dog and two cats, and driving a station wagon like all the other moms. But when I began to explore the possibilities of my own way of seeing things, my personal perception of the world, then I knew I had to write. Because although my experiences were similar to those of other people, no one had the same perception, the same feelings I had. Therefore, I had something to say. The trick was making them want to listen.

3. Clarity

If a writer doesn't know the story he's trying to tell, then an editor (and probably everyone else, except the writer's significant other!) will be confused by it. Clarity, even in a story with complex characters, can be achieved very easily by defining the structure, or bones, of the piece. Without a solid structure, even the most fascinating story will fall apart. It's like trying to build a house without a frame, or trying to walk around without a skeleton.

Let's take Shakespeare's *Hamlet*, for example. *Hamlet* is a great example of a well-structured play that revolves around a very complex character. Hamlet is told to avenge the murder of his father. He tries to do that. No one watching this play, or reading it, is in the dark about what Hamlet is trying to do (his goal or action), or even why he must do it (his motivation). However, Hamlet is probably the most complex character ever written, inspiring volumes of dissertations over the centuries. His complexity comes from the curious way he proceeds. But thanks to Shakespeare's crystal-clear story structure, we're never in the dark about what this story consists of.

Along with structure, clarity is also dependent upon knowing the theme of the piece you are writing. With nonfiction articles or books this is usually easy. *The Joy of Sex* is clearly about exactly what the title says. Alex Comfort wrote a best seller by sticking with his subject (sex) and his theme (joy), and never wavering.

Themes in fiction require the same kind of focus and understanding, although in the best fiction the author doesn't spell out the theme so bluntly. The theme is always at work in the background, though. Underneath the surface of the plot, or events of the story, *Hamlet* is about trying to understand the meaning of life and death. John Grisham's *The Firm* deals with the themes of greed and loyalty. *Gone with the Wind* is about women surviving in troubled times — with the deeper theme being, what is this thing called love.

Generally speaking, when a writer knows the subject inside and out, the story will be clear.

4. Simplicity

Perhaps the greatest challenge of a writer is to keep it simple: to write the words down the way they come to you, without judgment or vanity. If you're like most writers, you have an "inner critic" who wants you to write in order to impress someone. But it's pretty much guaranteed that if this is your primary motivation, you'll never achieve your goal. People who sit down to write a masterpiece usually never do it. Instead, their work appears as exactly what it is: stiff, self-conscious and uninspired.

When I sit down to write, I always tell myself that this is only an exercise. I can always change it, or destroy it. I'm only playing around with some ideas and some words. Soon my inner critic vanishes, and I'm off having a good time. I know that if I'm enjoying the writing, chances are the reader will too.

5. Passion

Good writing — writing that will attract a potential publisher — is written by someone who is passionate about their subject, their characters, and the human condition. Passion actually means "to suffer." I believe it was Dorothy Parker who said, "Writing is easy. Just sit down at the typewriter and open a vein." Sometimes remembering and feeling the pain of a past experience can be emotionally draining, even frightening. It can be thrilling and overwhelming — but it's the stuff of great fiction, and even good journalism, because it allows the reader to connect with the story, with the characters, and with your subject.

Even an article about making a peach pie will seem unappetizing if the writer isn't passionately involved with the taste of peaches. Anybody can write an aloof, factual account. What we all want is to know more, and hopefully, to feel more. We need writers who will help us do that.

6. Research

There's just no substitute for knowing what you're writing about. The best books and articles are usually those where the writer has taken the time to find out everything there is to know about the subject, and let the information distill in his brain.

Research is the perfect way to pack your writing with detail. Remember back in Chapter 3, where we talked about reading critically? There we discussed how the details in good writing make it interesting — how they separate a really exceptional book from a mediocre one. Take a look at a book you thoroughly enjoyed, and check out its descriptive passages. Chances are they're packed with visual details that made you feel like you were right there in the story. That level of detail is achieved by lots and lots of research!

Research is the perfect way to pack your writing with detail. In Chapter 18, we talk about reading critically. There we discuss how the details in good writing make it interesting — how they separate a really exceptional book from a mediocre one. Take a look at a book you thoroughly enjoyed, and check out its descriptive passages. Chances are they're packed with visual details that made you feel like you were right there in the story. That level of detail is achieved by lots and lots of research!

How To Market Your Writing

The marketing, and hopefully selling, of your writing, with the end result of seeing your work in print, is best accomplished by a strategic game plan. Beginning writers often practice the scattershot approach, sending to anyone and everyone. However, really researching the field of potential takers, and honestly assessing your own work will take you much further. Here are five steps you can take today that will really make a difference in your writing career!

1. Invest in *Writer's Market*

Writer's Market is an invaluable reference book, and a key source for getting your writing published. Usually libraries have a copy in the reference section, but if you can afford to buy your own, it is well worth the money. (At my local bookstore, it costs $26.99 plus tax.) A new edition comes out every year, so it contains the most up-to-date information about publishers you can find anywhere, with complete lists of all the periodicals, book publishers, and script publishers. There is even an extensive list of agents, Hollywood and otherwise. Its 1,000 pages are literally packed with information. *Writer's Market* could be the best investment you'll ever make in your writing career!

2. Write for Your Local Newspaper

Just about every town has a newspaper. Usually these are small publications that are actively looking for articles. Perhaps you're interested in writing theater reviews, or movie reviews. This is a marvelous way to become educated and to write at the same time.

The best news is that the movies and plays are free to reviewers! If you've never written a review before, study several in a larger newspaper, go to a film or a play, and then write a sample review to show the editor of your local newspaper. Before you know it, you could be seeing your name in print.

Or, perhaps you know everything about creating a French country garden, or Tex-Mex cooking, or you've got an idea for a series of humorous articles on raising children outdoors. One team of writers in Goleta, California started a successful column by recording and editing the local police blotter. It was very funny, and it was an article that people waited for and talked about every week.

If you want to write a series, start by writing a sample article. Accompany this with a letter explaining how you see your series taking shape over a period of six months. Send your letter and sample article to the appropriate editor at your local paper. After about a week, make a follow-up phone call to learn their reaction.

Writing reviews and articles for your local newspaper is no way to get rich quick. Most newspapers pay $20 per review — and if your newspaper is very small, your pay may be limited to free theater and movie tickets! Middle America newspapers pay between $25 and $100 per article. There are exceptions, though. If you're lucky you might develop an idea good enough for syndication in newspapers all across the country — and that means really big money for you!

But the whole point of writing for your local newspaper is to get practice and exposure, not to make a mint. You'll gain confidence as a writer and you'll gain the recognition of people in your community for your work. Plus, you'll accumulate a file of articles that you can then use as a stepping stone to bigger and better things!

3. Go to the Theater

If you are interested in writing plays, you should be reading lots of plays. You should also see every bit of live theater you can. All theaters are looking for people to usher. It's a great way to see free theater and to learn about playwriting because of the opportunity to see a play more than once. This is also a good way to meet actors. You can also try volunteering to help in other capacities at a theater, like helping backstage, or with the costumes, even building scenery. Once the actors know you, they may agree to read your play out loud in a group. Play readings with professional and semiprofessional actors is an invaluable experience. If the play works for them, the chance of having it performed is very likely. But always begin by treating them right. Invite them to your house and cook something really delicious to serve after the reading. Wine is good too. It will help you stop shaking, and smooth the edges of whatever criticism is forthcoming.

Plays can also be submitted to literary directors or artistic directors of most any theater. *The Dramatists Sourcebook* is an annual publication available at your local bookstore that lists all theaters and the appropriate people to approach. Again, a query letter is the best way to make an introduction.

4. Enter Writing Contests

Every year hundreds of contests are held to find new writers and to honor good writing. You can find an extensive list of these contests in *Writer's Market*. However, keep your ears open for contest opportunities in your immediate area. Local colleges and universities, as well as local newspapers and magazines, often hold contests for short fiction, poetry, and essay writing — and the winners of the contest usually get published. This is a very good way to break into print, and sometimes there's prize money as an extra added bonus.

One clear advantage you have in a contest is that older, professional writers generally do not enter contests, so your chances of winning are increased. Also, there is usually some community awareness surrounding contests — lots of people enter, lots of people read the winners, etc.

Contests for novels are an excellent way to get your manuscript read by a number of people, many of whom are actively looking for publishable works. Also, there is generally more than just one prize. Later, you can say you won the "Such & Such" Award, and you don't even have to tell what place you came in. Any contests or awards you win will only help you find and achieve the next publishing opportunity. And they may be the start of a great career, no matter how old you are. *Stones for Ibarra*, a lovely first novel by 74-year-old Harriet Doer, was the winner of a contest held by Stanford University. Her second novel, *Consider This, Señora*, was also very well received.

5. Join Writing Groups and Classes

There's no faster way to get yourself ahead in the publishing game than to educate yourself. Join writer's groups and attend writer's conferences — you'll find a list of writer's conferences in the back of this book. If you can't find a writer's group in your area, start your own by placing an ad in the paper, or put up a sign at the library or your neighborhood bookstore.

Find inexpensive or free adult education classes in writing at your local community college. Show up, pick the teacher's brain, talk with the other students. Write your heart out. Enter every local contest, and go to every party where there might be some artists or writers hanging around. Talk about your story, and pay attention to peoples' reactions. You'll know what to do as you go along. And one success will lead to another. In the meantime, you'll be having the time of your life! So get out there and go for it!

Professional Organizations

If you would like to join a professional writing organization for freelance writers, consider the American Society of Journalists and Authors, 1501 Broadway, Suite 302, New York City, New York 10036, (212) 997-0947. You must supply the Society with eight published reviews or writing clips to apply for membership.

166 Chapter 13: Get Your Own Writing Published!

There is also the National Book Critic's Circle, which moves its offices depending on the business address of its current president. (In 1995, this is Carlin Romano of the *Philadelphia Enquirer*). For membership information, contact Pat Holt, Book Editor at the *San Francisco Chronicle*.

For writers and those interested in specific publishing classes, there are Professional Writing Programs at over 100 college campuses nationwide. To order the *Official Guide to Writing Programs*, which costs $21.95, write George Mason University, Pallwood House, Mail Stop IE 3, Fairfax, Virginia 22030.

Chapter 14:
For Book Authors Only:
Finding an Agent

Maybe you have a great idea for a book—or maybe you've already written one, and are wondering, what next? There are basically two ways to go: approaching publishers on your own, like we described in Chapter 13; or finding an agent, and letting that agent approach the publishers for you.

The job of a literary agent is to match up writers like yourself with publishers who want to publish your book. It's not much different from a real estate agent who hooks up buyers and sellers. Just like selling a home tends to go much smoother when there's a real estate agent involved, selling a book to a publisher can go much smoother if you work with a literary agent. Of course, this service isn't free, so you must ask yourself the question…

Is It Worth It?

The literary agent makes money by taking 10 to 15% of the author's advance, which is money received up front when the book is sold to a publisher; plus, the agent gets 10% to 15% of the royalties, which is what the author makes on each copy of the book that's sold.

Now, you may be thinking: Wait a minute! I'm the author, and that's my money! True, but here's the rub: agents have a network of contacts in the publishing business that can't be beat. Having a good agent can dramatically reduce the length of time it takes to get your book published —

and a good agent can even make the difference between getting your book published and having it be lost in the slush pile forever.

Beating the Competition

The reality is, there are more publishers in this country than ever before, and more books are being published in this country than ever before. The catch is, more people are writing books than ever before, too! The larger publishers receive so many unsolicited manuscripts that they practically need warehouses to store them in!

An agent can give you the edge you need to break into this highly competitive field. On the other hand, you may do just as well approaching editors on your own. It partly depends on what kind of person you are, and what kind of book you are trying to sell. Also, some publishers will not accept "unagented" manuscripts — in which case, you don't have much choice!

This chapter will present the pros and cons of finding an agent so that you can decide what course of action is best for you.

Fiction Vs. Nonfiction

What kind of book are you writing — or, if you just have the idea right now, what kind of book do you want to write? Is it a romance novel or a how-to book on coin collecting? The answer to this question will help you decide whether to find an agent or not.

If you want to approach publishers on your own, it's much easier to do so with a nonfiction book than a fiction book. Nonfiction books include how-to books, cookbooks, business books, travel books, true crime stories, and other books about specific topics — from science books and "pop" psychology books to books on religion, gardening, crafts, race cars, computers, and just about any other subject you can name.

Why do novels and short stories do better with agents? Judging fiction is a very subjective business — and it just so happens that agents are experts at making judgment calls about works of fiction. Publishers can rely on good agents to send them good books. And because so much fiction is being written these days, publishers have come to rely on agents to provide them with a built-in screening process.

Because of this, agents are VERY particular about the authors and books they take on. Representing just one clunker will give the agent a bad reputation in the publishing world. That means YOU must put your very best foot forward in order to join an agent's stable of writers! We'll show you how later in this chapter.

The Role of an Agent

The best agents will take your book manuscript under their wing and help you polish it to perfection. If they see a diamond in the rough, they will help you uncover it, and then they will do everything in their power to turn it into a best seller!

Here's a true story about a psychologist who had an idea for a book — but really didn't know how to write it. A writer friend who had an agent put the two of them in touch. The agent was interested in her idea and asked her to send what she had. She sent in piles of unorganized material, but the agent saw its potential. He helped the psychologist get the manuscript in shape, and it went on to become a national best seller!

The key elements of the story are these: the agent saw that the manuscript had potential — BIG potential — because it was based on an idea he could sell. Plus, the psychologist was well established in her field and really knew her subject, inside and out. With nonfiction, it always helps if your book is about a subject you really know.

But didn't we just say that you don't really need an agent for a nonfiction book? Yes, we did. The exception to this is if you have a REALLY hot book idea — one with best seller potential that might involve movie deals, foreign rights, and sales of other products that are related to the book. If you have reason to believe your book is that hot, by all means, shop for an agent right away!

How to Find An Agent

The very best way for a beginning writer to find an agent is through personal contacts. That's where all the networking we've talked about throughout this book comes in.

For example, you might meet an agent at a writer's conference that you attended after reading the list in the back of this book. You might meet other writers in a class through Adult Education or your local college, and one of those writers might have an agent. You might be talking to a friend one day, and find out that they can put you in touch with a writer friend of theirs who has an agent. Don't forget to join local writer's groups and national organizations of writers that relate to your area of interest — they are also great sources of contacts and information regarding agents! See the list of national organizations in the back of this book for ideas.

While you're looking for an agent, your book can benefit greatly from these classes, writer's groups, and conferences. You will have the chance to share parts of your book with many other individuals, who will have many useful suggestions for ways you can improve your work.

Always remember to present yourself sincerely and honestly in whatever situation you find yourself. Don't be too pushy. Instead, be very courteous and be willing to learn from everyone you meet. Ask questions and listen carefully to the answers. Make a good impression, and people will want to help you out!

If you really want to find an agent, there's simply no substitute for a personal referral. Be polite and persistent, and you will find one!

The Next Best Thing: Go Shopping

The next best thing to a personal referral is to go shopping for an agent. In fact, we recommend that you do both simultaneously!

You can begin with the sample list of 35 agents at the end of this chapter. Keep in mind that there are approximately 1,000 literary agencies and literary agents in this country! You can find many more names of agents in that famous resource book we keep talking about, the *Literary Market Place*. Yet another source is the *1995 Writer's Digest Guide to Literary Agents*, available from Writer's Digest Books (1-800-289-0963), which includes over 400 listings of agents who represent writers of books, TV shows, and movies. Also, check for listings of agents in the trusty Yellow Pages of your phone book. Between these four sources, you'll have plenty of material for your shopping spree!

The Query Letter

Start off on the right foot by selecting only those agents who will consider the type of book you are writing! The usual procedure is to send a query letter first, with a self-addressed, stamped envelope. The self-addressed, stamped envelope is very important. In fact, many agents will throw your letter away unless it has one!

Make sure your letter is very professional. Be sure to type it and use very good paper, and good envelopes too. Do not send photocopies of the same query letter; instead, personalize each letter for each agent.

Finally, DO NOT send your manuscript unless the agent asks to see it! Most agents will not even read manuscripts that arrive on their doorstep unless they have seen and responded to a query letter first.

Save yourself the agony and the postage of mailing out your manuscript to dozens of agents — instead, put your energy into writing the very best query letter that you can! The query letter is your sales pitch, your big chance to get your foot in the door.

Entire books have been written on the art of the query letter. One of the best is *How to Write Irresistible Query Letters* from Writer's Digest Books. Basically your query letter must be short and to the point — no more than a page or a page and a half long. The query letter must contain these four basic elements:

- A "hook" at the beginning, to catch the agent's interest and let him know what your subject is about.

- For a nonfiction book, some statistics or other supporting material to validate why your book is needed. For a fiction book, an exciting capsule summary of the plot.

- Brief biographical information about yourself. Why are you qualified to write this book?

- A conclusion where you ask for a speedy response and thank the agent for their time.

Here's a sample query letter to get you started:

Today's Date

Andrew Agent
555 Publishing Way
Any City, USA 88990

Dear Andrew Agent:

One of the biggest challenges for single people today is finding that special someone—someone who can be a partner in a lasting, meaningful relationship. Singles spend over $1.5 billion every year answering personal ads, joining dating services, and using computer bulletin boards, all in an effort to find Ms. or Mr. Right.

And while many books have been written on this subject, few of them can promise methods that really work. My book will change all of that.

How to Meet, Win, and Keep the Love of Your Life in 30 Days or Less shows readers how to succeed in love, once and for all! My methods have been tested and proven by over 200 people in Anytown, USA. Over 80% of these people are now happily married.

I myself am now happily married by using the unique 30-day plan outlined in this book. After having been single for nearly 15 years, I finally had enough and set out to change all that. I developed a foolproof system to cure myself of being single, and then set out to share my techniques with others. I have taught a class called "How to Meet, Win and Keep the Love of Your Life" in Anytown's Adult Education Program for the past three years—and it is one of the most successful classes in the entire history of the program.

The class is successful because the method really works. It really IS possible to meet, win, and keep the love of your life in 30 days or less! I believe this book will be the next best seller in this huge market.

Thank you for your prompt attention to this proposal. I look forward to your response.

Sincerely,

Mary Matchmaker
222 Lovebird Lane
Anytown, USA 21112

A Word to the Wise: No Phone Calls

Agents like query letters for a reason. They are able to read them on their own time and carefully consider their response. By all means, resist the temptation to call agents and tell them about your great book idea over the phone.

Most agents are besieged by people who are literally beating down their doors for the chance to be published. Don't become one of the mob — instead, set yourself apart by writing a courteous, professional query letter! By doing so, you'll be giving the agents the professional respect that they deserve.

The only time you might even consider calling an agent is if you have a personal referral from a friend of theirs, or from another writer who they represent. Even then, you can expect the agent to say something like, "Great, I'd be happy to consider your idea. Please send me a query letter and I'll get back to you."

After you send your query letter, DO NOT call to find out the agent's reaction to it. You risk being labeled as a pest if you do and being ignored forever! As long as you've enclosed a self-addressed, stamped envelope, you can expect to receive a reply in two weeks to two months. Just be patient, and send out your query to more than one agent at once to improve your odds of getting a positive response!

A Word About Small-Time Agents

You might be able to find a small-time agent through word of mouth. Agents who are just starting out may not have a big track record — and they oftentimes don't belong to the Association of Author's Representatives — but some of them will work extra hard for you and get results!

How can you tell if a small-time agent is any good? Well, start out by asking for personal references. Then, trust your feelings. Small-time agents may be a gamble, but if they have connections that can benefit your particular book, it may be worth the risk.

If you've put in some time trying to interest a big-time agent without success, don't ignore the opportunities presented by a small-time agent.

What About Agents Who Advertise?

A word of caution: be wary of agents who take out ads in writer's magazines. While some of these people may be legitimate, a fair number of them make their money by charging you a fee up front — and then doing nothing to help sell your manuscript!

On the other hand, the agents who appear in *Literary Market Place* and in the list at the end of this chapter are all members of the Association of Author's Representatives, which is the leading professional organization for literary agents in the U.S. Members of this organization do not charge up-front fees to authors for reading or evaluating your manuscript.

If you do decide to respond to an agent's advertisement, be sure to ask for referrals — and check these references carefully. Then meet the agent in person. Do you like him or her? What's your gut feeling—do you trust this person to go to bat for you?

What About Reading Fees?

Some reputable literary agents do charge reading fees. A reasonable fee is $25 to $75 for reading a complete manuscript. In exchange for your money, you get a critique with constructive comments. This critique may be well worth it to you—though if you're in a writing class or writing group, you probably have plenty of opportunities to get your work critiqued already that don't cost you anything!

Some of the more shady literary agents may try to get you to fork over as much as $300 or more to read your manuscript. Beware of these individuals! Oftentimes they are just reading services disguised as literary agencies. They may have no contacts available to help you get your book published, even if they say they like the manuscript.

We recommend that you save your money and use it for something else that could benefit you more — for example, to attend a writer's conference where you'll meet some real agents in person!

Don't Forget the Internet!

Another way to find an agent is the modern, computerized way: through your home computer. I personally know a writer who found a New York agent by joining a computer writer's forum on the Internet.

How does it work? First, you must find a local Internet provider. Your local library will usually have the names of these — or, try calling a local computer store or university computer center. Once you're on the Net, scan the possible categories. My friend found a writer's forum by entering her geographic area, then choosing the category "arts," and then specifying "writers." Then she was able to talk with other writers via electronic mail—and it turned out one of the other writers referred her to his own agent, and allowed her to use his name as a reference!

If for some reason you can't get access to the Internet, join the Writer's Forum on America Online or Compuserve. These forums are very active and you may have great success there as well!

Hallelujah, They Said Yes!

Someday soon that magic day will arrive when one of those SASEs appears in your mailbox with a short note from an agent that says, "Liked your query letter. Please send more information ASAP."

If you're writing a fiction book, the agent will usually want to see the entire manuscript. If you're writing a nonfiction book, the agent will want to see a book proposal and perhaps a sample chapter.

A nonfiction book proposal consists of the following elements: an overview of your book, a biography of yourself, an evaluation of your book's competition, and an outline of each chapter. The average book proposal is 15–30 double-spaced, typed pages. But proposals can be as short as five pages — it all depends on the nature of your book!

There are many books available that will give you guidance on writing book proposals. One of them is *Write the Perfect Book Proposal* by Jeff Herman and Deborah M. Adams (John Wiley & Sons, Inc., 1993). Look for it at your library or bookstore.

After the agent reviews your manuscript or proposal, they will decide whether or not to take you on as a new author. If you make the cut, soon the agent will be presenting your book to different publishers, and negotiating deals on your behalf. And next thing you know, you'll be depositing a big fat advance in the bank, with royalties on their way that could last for years to come!

And Now For the Agents!

Here, then, are the names of 35 agents with their areas of interest. Remember the ground rules: no phone calls; send a query letter; and always present yourself in a professional manner. Review this chapter if you have any questions about how to approach an agent. And best of luck to you!

Acton, Dystel, Leone and Jaffe
79 Fifth Ave.
New York, NY 10003
Nonfiction: current events, politics, history, biography, science, health and medicine, women's issues, parenting, sports, cookbooks, business, social issues, inspirational.
Fiction: literary, romance, women's commercial, men's thrillers.

Agency Chicago
PO Box 11200
Chicago, IL 60611
Nonfiction: travel, sports, history, true crime.

Lee Allen Agency
Box 18617
Milwaukee, WI 53218
Fiction: science fiction, fantasy, mystery, horror, thrillers, men's adventure, historical, westerns.

Loretta Barrett Books, Inc.
101 Fifth Ave.
New York, NY 10003
Nonfiction: psychology, New Age, women's issues. Fiction: women's fiction, mysteries, thrillers.

Daniel Bial Agency
41 West 83rd St. 5-C
New York, NY 10024
Nonfiction: business, sports, history, psychology, humor, cooking, reference, science.
Fiction: adventure, mysteries.

The Joan Brandt Agency
788 Wesley Dr. NW
Atlanta, GA 30305
Nonfiction: popular or topical.
Fiction: detective, police, mystery, crime, contemporary issues.

Patti Breitman
12 Rally Court
Fairfax, CA 94930
Nonfiction: health, food, parenting, human growth, animal rights, business, spirituality, vegetarianism.
Fiction: none.

Andrea Brown Literary Agency, Inc.
PO Box 429
El Granada, CA 94018
Children's books, historical romance, science fiction.

Julie Castiglia Literary Agency
1155 Camino Del Mar
Suite 510
Del Mar, CA 92014

Nonfiction: psychology, science and health, biography, women's issues, contemporary issues.
Fiction: literary, ethnic, and mainstream.

Francine Ciske Literary Agency
PO Box 555
Neenah, WI 54957
Children's books, science fiction/fantasy, poetry, short story collections.

Ruth Cohen, Inc.
PO Box 7626
Menlo Park, CA 94025
Fiction: women's fiction, historical romances, Regency romances, genre mysteries.
Children's books: picture books, middle grade fiction/nonfiction, young adults.

Richard Curtis Associates, Inc.
171 East 74th St.
New York, NY 10021
Nonfiction: multimedia electronic works for computer.
Fiction: science fiction, thrillers, romances.

Joyce A. Flaherty, Literary Agent
816 Lynda Court
St. Louis, MO 63122
Nonfiction: self-help, investigative reporting, Americana.
Fiction: women's fiction, thrillers.

The Fogelman Literary Agency
7515 Greenville Ave., Suite 712
Dallas, TX 75231
Nonfiction: popular business, self-help, biographies, true crime.
Fiction: romances, especially Regency romances; also mysteries and women's fiction.

Bill Gladstone
Waterside Productions, Inc.
2191 San Elijo Ave.
Cardiff-by-the-Sea, CA 92007
Nonfiction: how-to computer books, game books, business, biographies, general how-to.

Heacock Literary Agency, Inc.
1523 Sixth St., Suite 14
Santa Monica, CA 90401
Nonfiction: diet, health, nutrition, exercise, popular psychology, women's studies, alternative health, sports, celebrity biographies.

Hull House Literary Agency
240 East 82nd St.
New York, NY 10028
Nonfiction: biography, true crime, military history, books on arts.
Fiction: crime novels, commercial fiction.

Natasha Kern Literary Agency, Inc.
PO Box 2908
Portland, OR 97208
Nonfiction: health, science, feminism, parenting, psychology, self-help, true crime, current issues, celebrity biographies, business, reference.
Fiction: women's fiction, romances, historical novels, thrillers, mysteries.

Michael Larsen/Elizabeth Pomada Literary Agents
1029 Jones St.
San Francisco, CA 94109
Nonfiction: business, popular science, psychology, food, biographies, true crime, how-to.
Fiction: thrillers, romances, mysteries, literary novels.

Toni Lopopolo Literary Agency
PO Box 1494
Manhattan Beach, CA 90244
Nonfiction: child rearing, family economics, biography, Americana, history.
Fiction: crime, Westerns, mysteries, horror.

March Tenth, Inc.
4 Myrtle St.
Haworth, NJ 07641
Music, popular culture, biographies.

Ruth Nathan Literary Agency
80 Fifth Ave., Room 706
New York, NY 10011
Nonfiction: art, decorative arts, show business, true crime.

New England Publishing Associates, Inc.
PO Box 5
Chester, CT 06412
Nonfiction: women's subjects, biographies, true crime, current affairs, reference, history, self-help.

Edward A. Novak III Literary Representation
711 North Second St., Suite 1
Harrisburg, PA 17102
Nonfiction: sports, business/legal, memoirs, history.
Fiction: romances.

Oriole Literary Agency
2065 Arnold Way, Suite 103B
Alpine, CA 91901
Nonfiction: business, celebrity biographies, current events/politics, sports, fitness, true crime.
Fiction: police-related fiction or military fiction only.

James Peter Associates, Inc.
PO Box 772
Tenafly, NJ 07670
Nonfiction only: history, popular culture, politics, business, biography, popular health and psychology, social issues, popular reference, how-to.

Pesha Rubinstein Literary Agency, Inc.
37 Overlook Terrace #1D
New York, NY 10033
Fiction: Women's fiction, romances, mysteries, horror, thrillers, children's picture books.

The Russell-Simenauer Literary Agency, Inc.
PO Box 43267
14 Capron Lane
Upper Montclair, NJ 07043
Nonfiction: how-to, self-help, women's issues, parenting, recovery, health, fitness, medical, diet, nutrition. Also true crime,

business, sports, celebrities, specialized cookbooks.
Fiction: mysteries, thrillers, historical novels, humorous.

The Seymour Agency
7 Rensselaer Ave.
Heuvelton, NY 13654
Nonfiction: outdoors books.
Fiction: women's fiction, historical romance, contemporary romance, Regency romance, suspense/thriller.

Michael Snell Literary Agency
PO Box 1206
Truro, MA 02666
Nonfiction: business books, self-help, how-to, computer books.
Fiction: literary fiction, suspense, mysteries.

Elyse Sommer, Inc.
110-34 73rd Rd.
PO Box 75133
Forest Hills, NY 11375
Reference books.

Stepping Stone Literary Agency
59 West 71st St., Suite 9B
New York, NY 10023

Nonfiction: women's issues, men's issues, mind/body health issues, travel, art books, cookbooks, psychology.
Fiction: love stories.

Susan P. Urstadt, Inc.
Writers and Artists Agency
103 Brushy Ridge Rd.
New Canaan, CT 06840
Nonfiction: history, biography, food and wine, gardening, art, antiques, decorative arts, natural science, travel, education, health, careers.
Fiction: quality commercial fiction.

The Wallace Literary Agency
177 East 70th St.
New York, NY 10021
Nonfiction: history, politics, biography, memoirs, sports, current events, travel.

Susan Zeckendorf Associates, Inc.
171 West 57th St., Suite 11B
New York, NY 10019
Nonfiction: history, biography, music, psychology, science.
Fiction: mysteries, thrillers, women's fiction.

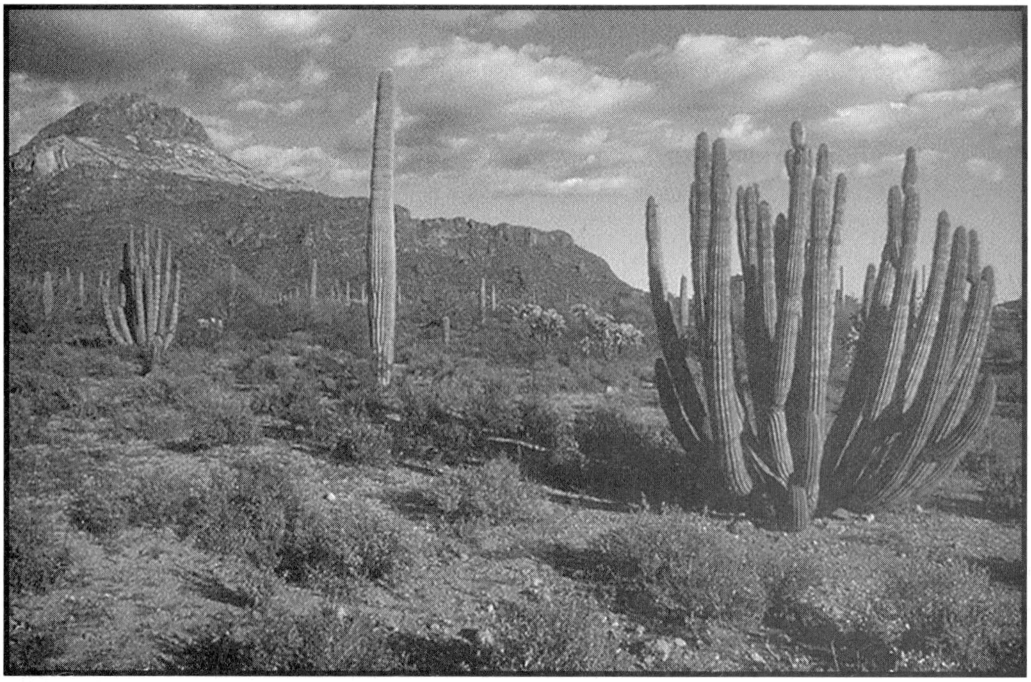

Chapter 15: Writing Children's Books

If you've always wondered whether you could write children's books, this chapter is especially for you. Maybe you've spent long hours reading to your own kids and thought, "I could write books like this!" Maybe you've even tried your hand at a few stories.

This chapter will show you the basics about one of the most delightful markets that exists for your writing. Luckily, it also turns out that the children's book market is one of the most approachable markets in the publishing world. The novice writer — that is, a writer without an agent who has never published a book before — actually has a decent chance of breaking into the children's book market. This is not true of many other areas in the publishing world, where it can take years and lots of blood, sweat, and tears before you see results.

The Society of Children's Book Writers

One of the most helpful organizations in the country in this field is the Society of Children's Book Writers and Illustrators, which has been a guiding force in the industry for over twenty years. Composed of authors, publishers, editors, agents, librarians and others professionally involved in the children's book world, the SCBWI also welcomes beginning writers or those who are simply interested in the field.

Beginning writers can join as Associate Members, while already published writers join as Full Members. Both types of membership have the same great benefits. (The only difference is that Associate Members do not have a vote on the organization's board of directors.)

For a membership application, write the SCBWI at 22736 Vanowen St., Suite 106, West Hills, CA 91307. Enclose a self-addressed, stamped envelope and a brief letter saying that you would like them to send you a membership application and a brochure about SCBWI. There is a $50 annual membership fee, which is tax deductible — and it could be the best investment you ever made! This is one organization that gives you a lot for your money. Read on to learn more.

SCBWI Supports New Writers

The SCBWI — which is staffed by volunteer authors — has as its mission to mentor and nurture a new generation of authors, as well as supporting those already in the field. Each year a half a dozen grants are given to members to help them complete specific book projects. Regional Advisors coordinate events for members in locations all over the country. These meetings and workshops feature well-known writers, illustrators, and others involved in literature for young people.

Several different publications, designed to aid both published and unpublished writers, are available to SCBWI members for the cost of postage only. These include pamphlets on all aspects of the trade and a bimonthly magazine for members that offers an update on the market — who is buying what — and all sorts of other timely information. Inquire about these publications when you write the address given above for your membership application.

The society also offers the annual Golden Kite Awards for best written and illustrated books of the year. This is one of the most prestigious awards in the country for children's books. Yes, there's no doubt about it — the list of benefits you receive from belonging to SCBWI is practically endless! And one of the best of all is the...

SCBWI Annual Conference

Every August the SCBWI hosts a four-day conference in Marina del Rey, California. This is the only conference in the country that is devoted entirely to writing and illustrating books for children. It draws hundreds of children's book professionals every year.

The conference is a wonderful introduction to the world of children's books. It gives you a chance to network with other writers and attend readings, critique sessions, and lectures on all aspects of the trade. You'll learn how the children's book business works and make the necessary contacts to further your budding career.

If you have a manuscript, you can submit it for a personalized critique session, which is usually a half-hour session where you meet face-to-face with a professional writer or editor. Now, there's no better way to improve your writing and increase your chances of being published than to have your work read by someone who's already established in the field! If you can take advantage of an opportunity like this, by all means do so! Find out more by writing the SCBWI at the address given above, and be sure to enclose a self-addressed stamped envelope.

Why Did They Do It?

You might wonder why the Society of Children's Book Writers and Illustrators took it upon themselves to single-handedly create a support network for children's writers on a national scale.

Let's call it pride. When the Society was formed twenty years ago, children's book authors were the black sheep of the publishing industry — looked down upon, not respected. The general attitude was that "anyone" could write children's books, that it was not a professional's market, and when were these authors going to grow up and start writing books for adults anyway?

To bring self-esteem to the children's book market, the pioneers who created SCBWI created a professional network of friends to raise industry standards and improve the perception of children's books. Their goal was to nurture the trade by looking out for each other and developing easy-to-use guidelines for novice writers. And they did it all so well that now you can benefit from their success!

Tips from a Pro

Lee Wardlaw, a noted children's author who offers workshops on various aspects of breaking into the children's book market, cannot speak more highly of the SCBWI. She also had some other suggestions for newcomers to the market.

The Institute of Children's Literature is a correspondence school that offers extremely helpful feedback and training to its students. Now you might wonder if a correspondence or "mail-in" school would be legitimate, but we were assured that this one is — the quality of the instructors who critique student's manuscripts is very high. The Institute also publishes a magazine for children's writers. Request more information by writing:

Institute of Children's Literature
95 Long Ridge Road
West Redding, Connecticut 06896

Writer's Conferences

There are two writer's conferences that are especially respected and helpful to children's book writers. The Highlights Foundation Writers Conference in Chautauqua, New York — presented by Highlights for Children, the famous magazine for kids — offers 10 days of seminars and classes where the instructors will work with you day in and day out. If you submit a manuscript ahead of time, an author or editor will offer you a personal critique session. For information on the conference, write to:

Highlights for Children, Dept. CWL
814 Court Street
Honesdale, Pennsylvania 18431

For more advanced students and professionals in the field, there is the Port Townsend Writer's Conference (known as "Centrum") presented annually in Port Townsend, Washington. This is a hot conference where experienced writers go for seminars and workshops, readings and lectures as well as invaluable networking. See Appendix A in the back of this book for contact information on this and other conferences.

Seek Out Local Classes

Most university extension or adult education programs at community colleges offer classes in writing children's books. There are also authors and lecturers like Lee Wardlaw who travel widely and offer seminars on various aspects of breaking into the children's book market.

Wardlaw travels mostly around the West Coast and offers classes on different genres — picture books, nonfiction, novels for juveniles, etc. If you are interested in Lee Wardlaw's seminars, send a self-addressed postcard requesting schedule information to her at P.O. Box 1452, Summerland, CA 93067.

For additional workshops and seminars, check the listings in Appendix A of this book.

Children's Writer's and Illustrator's Market

An invaluable source book widely referred to in the children's book publishing industry is the *Children's Writers' and Illustrators' Market*, edited by Lisa Carpenter and published by Writer's Digest Books. The book lists children's book and magazine publishers, offers personal "close-ups" of successful writers and illustrators, and has a big section on the business of children's writing and illustrating, including information on formats for submission, researching markets, agents, contracts and royalties, insurance, taxes, rights, etc.

Children's Writers' and Illustrators' Market is readily available in bookstores and at library reference desks. You can also order it direct from the publisher for $19.99 by calling 1-800-289-0963. Writer's Digest Books also offers these other titles of special interest to children's book authors. Look for them at your library or order them by calling the toll-free number:

- *How to Write and Sell Children's Picture Books*, by Jean E. Karl, $16.95

- *Writing for Children and Teenagers*, by Lee Wyndam and Arnold Madison, $12.95

- *How to Write and Illustrate Children's Books*, edited by Treld Pelkey Bicknell and Felicity Trotman, $22.50

Get to Know the Market

We can't say it often enough: your first step to success is getting to know the children's book market. This means finding out what book publishers and magazines might be interested in your work by actually reading what they publish. The worst thing you can do is send a manuscript of your own to a publisher without ever looking at the books they've actually published. Why?

Believe us, the publisher will be able to tell immediately from your cover letter that you have no idea what they are looking for. Even worse, if you send yet another manuscript, you will have cast your bad reputation in concrete. And it's practically impossible to undo that kind of damage.

Finding the right publishing house is like finding the right husband or wife. There are many potential mates out there, but you must learn a great deal about someone before you say "I do." The more you know about a publishing house, the greater the chances are that they will say "I do" to you, and your book or story will get published!

Find the Publishers You Like

A good tactic is to ask yourself, who publishes my favorite children's books? Write down the names of those publishers and then look them up. There are three sources you can use to find the names and addresses of publishers: *Children's Writer's and Illustrator's Market; The Literary Market Place;* and *Writer's Market.*

Next, write letters to the publishers whose books you like and ask them to send you their writer's guidelines. Every publisher has specific guidelines for submissions, and you must know what they are BEFORE you send in your manuscript.

If you come across a book publisher you want to know more about, ask your bookstore or library to help you find books published by that specific company. If it's a magazine publisher, look at copies of the magazine at your bookstore or library. If copies aren't available at those places, you can write the publisher and ask them to send you a sample copy. Be sure to enclose a self-addressed stamped envelope with your letter and ask to receive the magazine's writer's guidelines as well.

Keep a list of the publishers you like, and when you get writer's guidelines from each one, file them away. You'll be building your own reference system of publishers you'd be proud to be associated with. That alone will inspire you to write even more and then decide which of your books, stories, and articles to submit to each one.

How to Approach a Publisher

Every publisher is different. That's why it's so important to consult reference guides like the *Children's Writer's and Illustrator's Market*. These guides will tell you whether the publisher wants you to send your entire manuscript with a cover letter, or whether they prefer you to send just a query letter first. Also, they will give you the names of specific editors that you'll need in order to address your letters and manuscripts to the right person. (Note: these reference guides are updated every year, so be sure you use this year's edition — the publishers and their personnel can change quite a bit from year to year!)

Generally speaking, most publishers prefer a query letter for nonfiction books, whereas for fiction they prefer to see the complete manuscript (accompanied by a cover letter). If you need help writing a query letter, Writer's Digest Books publishes a great book called *How to Write Irresistible Query Letters*. There's also a sample query letter in this book in Chapter 14.

The cover letter you send with a complete fiction manuscript should do three things: it should introduce you to the publisher, mention any credentials you already have as a writer, and give the editor an overview of the manuscript. See the sample cover letter in Chapter 13.

Don't Forget the SASE

Here's an important note on sending in your manuscripts. Always include a self-addressed manila envelope large enough to hold your manuscript, and make sure it has the correct postage. The publisher must be able to return your manuscript, or it will simply be thrown away! The point is, if they don't publish it, you can use that copy of your manuscript to send to someone else!

A Market with a Heart

The best thing about the market for children's books is that it really does have a heart. Remember, this is one area of the publishing industry where the "slush piles" of unsolicited manuscripts are actually read. This is also an industry where there are plenty of opportunities to learn from the pros — from classes, seminars, conferences, and critique sessions to the information provided by the Society of Children's Book Writers and Illustrators.

Last, but not least, don't forget to read widely in the field of children's books. By doing so you'll have lots of fun, for one thing — and you'll also learn a great deal about different styles of writing. You'll discover the genres or styles of writing that are best suited to you, and you'll be inspired to create your own stories that will make their way out into the world. As a children's book writer, you have the opportunity to educate young people and to bring smiles to the faces of many people, young and old. It's a noble calling, and we wish you all the best with it!

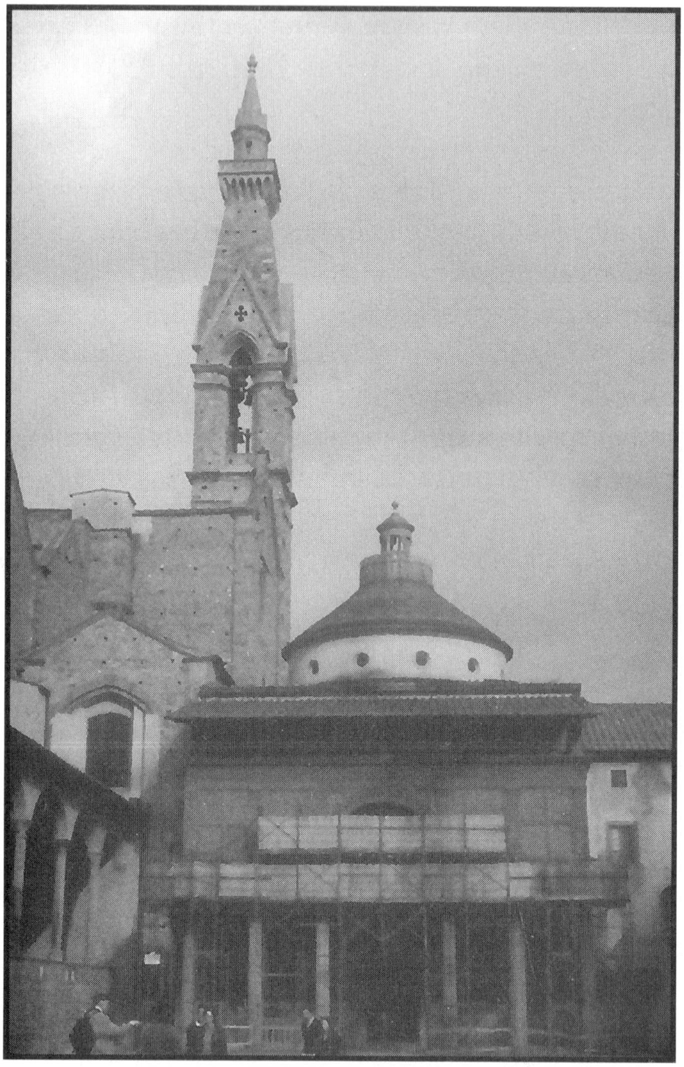

Chapter 16: Writing for Magazines

Do you love magazines? Do you subscribe to them, buy them at supermarkets and bookstores, and devour their contents? Do you ever think to yourself, "I have an idea for an article that I know would be just perfect for this magazine!" If so, read on!

There is a huge market out there for people interested in writing for magazines. Take a look at the list of magazines in *Writer's Market*. There are 600 pages of magazine listings! Not only are there the magazines you see every day in supermarkets and bookstores — the so-called "consumer magazines"—but there are a great many more magazines known as trade journals. These business, technical, and professional journals focus on news relevant to a particular occupation or industry. Whatever field you work in at the present time, you can probably find several trade journals that would be only too happy to hear from you!

This chapter will give you the basics of what it takes to write for magazines. There's a starter list of magazines in Volume II. Armed with that and a copy of *Writer's Market* (which you can get at your local library or bookstore), you'll be ready to enter this very rewarding field!

Success Secrets

The entire secret of writing and selling successful magazine articles is to understand the magazine's audience. It helps if you already read the magazine regularly yourself. If you don't, get your hands on several recent issues and read them carefully! You can find recent issues of magazines at your library, bookstore, or by writing the magazine and requesting sample copies.

What will you learn from this exercise? You'll discover the kinds of articles the magazine actually publishes. You'll see how long the articles usually are, and you'll get a feeling for the magazine's "editorial focus" — which simply means, what the editors like to print and how they like the articles to sound. You'll also become familiar with the magazine's "departments" — which are columns of information that appear in every issue. One of the best ways to break in to a magazine is to write a short piece for one of the regular departments.

There's another advantage you'll have by reading back issues of the magazine. You'll find out if they've already done an article on the idea you're thinking about! In fact, before you submit a story idea, try to find out if they've done anything similar in the past year. One of the easiest ways to check a year of back issues is at your local library.

Get the Writer's Guidelines

Most magazines have writer's guidelines for the asking. Simply write the publication and request them. These guidelines will give you very specific instructions about how to prepare your article for publication. I can't emphasize enough the importance of following these guidelines. Most editors will simply throw your article in the circular file if you haven't taken the trouble to get them!

At the same time you request the writer's guidelines, ask for an editorial calendar. This will tell you the magazine's editorial plan for the year. You'll find out the theme for each issue and also about any upcoming special issues. All this is invaluable information for you when it comes to deciding which of your articles to send out, and when!

Magazine editors are always complaining about writers who send the wrong submissions to their magazines. By reading the magazine and asking for the writer's guidelines, you'll be two steps ahead of the game — and you'll dramatically increase your chances of being published!

Write About What You Know

Here's a success secret that seems pretty obvious when you think about it — though it's one many writers tend to forget. Write about what you know. What do you know more about than other people? What do you do better than most other people you know? What are your hobbies and interests? What topics could you write about that are related to your job?

Everyone is an expert on something — whether it's baking brownies, hitting a home run, or understanding the new accounts receivable system at your office. Believe me, people out in the world want to hear about how you do what you do!

Right now, make a list of ten things that you know how to do well. Next to each one, list three potential article ideas that are based on each thing you do well. This list will be your starting point for writing successful magazine articles!

Write About What You Love

Here's yet another success secret: write about what you love. Maybe you love your kids, your church, your cats. Maybe you have other talents too that are harder to measure, like being able to comfort other people in their time of need. Or maybe you've overcome a difficult illness, or conquered obstacles in a way that would be inspiring to others. Writing about whatever you love will make a great magazine article — an article that people will read from start to finish!

So right now, get out another piece of paper and list ten things that you love. Next to each one, list three potential article ideas that are based on each thing that you love. You'll have more article ideas than you know what to do with!

Writing Can Be Fun!

When you think about it, why would you even want to consider writing about a topic you don't know anything about, or a topic that you don't even like? There's nothing to be gained by suffering through writing a magazine article as though it were a homework assignment at school. Writing can be fun — and it WILL be fun if you stick to these two success secrets! Magazine editors will recognize your talent and enthusiasm, and readers will appreciate that you took the trouble to share what you know with them!

The Query Letter

Remember those writer's guidelines you sent away for? Now it's time to get them out and see what each magazine's policy is about query letters.

Generally speaking, most magazine editors want to see a query letter for a full-length article before you send it in. On the other hand, short items for the department sections of a magazine can often be submitted without a query letter. Query letters are actually a good thing for you, because you don't waste your time writing the entire article only to find out that the magazine can't use it! Instead, you use the query letter to sell them on the idea of the article.

Whatever the magazine's policy about query letters, be sure to follow it exactly. If you need to write a query letter, make sure it includes the following items: your topic, your research sources, the length of the article, and when you can submit the completed article. Here is a sample query letter that you can adapt for your specific needs.

Today's Date

Everett Editor
Gardening Tools Magazine
555 Publishing Blvd.
Any City, USA

Dear Everett Editor:

As a long-time subscriber to *Gardening Tools Magazine*, I look forward to receiving each and every issue. I have a half-acre garden myself, and I have always found the magazine's advice about garden tools to be very useful to me.

I am also a freelance writer, and I would like to propose the following idea for a feature article in your magazine. This article, titled "Don't Call a Spade a Spade," explains why not all spades are created equal. In fact, through research at the Gardening Institute of America, I discovered that there are no fewer than 20 different kinds of spades!

This 2,000 word article will give a brief, user-friendly description of what each kind of spade is used for. The article will conclude with the latest development in spade technology, the brand new high-grade steel spade that puts all its ancestors to shame.

I am a regular contributor to *Everything's Coming Up Roses*, the newsletter of Anytown Garden Club. A sample of my writing is enclosed. I could have "Don't Call a Spade a Spade" ready by June 1. I look forward to hearing from you soon.

Sincerely,

Gerry Gardener
77 Rototiller Lane
Anytown, USA 55667
456-444-3333

Query Letter Dos and Don'ts

- DO make your query sound interesting. A query letter is a sales letter. Make the editor want to buy your article!

- DON'T ask editors for advice of any kind. Instead, TELL them how you're going to write the article.

- DO keep your query letter to one page if at all possible — certainly no longer than 1 ½ pages. Type the letter and use single spacing.

- DO address the query to the right editor and spell that editor's name correctly.

- DO double-check your query letter for typos and grammar mistakes.

- DON'T use flowery stationery or any stationery other than good quality, 8 ½ × 11 bond paper.

- DON'T include an SASE with your query letter. A query letter is business correspondence and it will be treated as such by the editors.

- DON'T boast about important editors you have known.

- DON'T try to get attention with decals or brightly colored envelopes. These things will get attention all right, but not the kind you want!

- DON'T put opinions in your query letter, either your own or someone else's.

- DON'T make telephone queries. Always put your query in writing!

Set Your Goals

The next step in your success plan for writing magazine articles is to set a goal for each article. What is the article's purpose? Is it to educate your readers, or to entertain them? Will your article help people make money, be healthier, improve their skills, or understand a difficult subject? Or will you provide an insight into the trials and triumphs of everyday life?

Once you have a clear goal in mind, you're ready to sit down and write your article. How will you explain your topic in a way that makes sense? Usually you'll need a combination of informative facts about your subject, plus examples or anecdotes to illustrate the point you are making. You might do some research at your local library to get the facts, or you might interview people who have the answers. Depending on the kind of article you are writing, you might be able to draw your examples from personal experience, or from the experience of people you know.

Sit Down to Write!

Now that you've done your research, it's time to actually sit down and write the article! Keep your sample copies of the magazine handy as you write. Try to imitate the style of the magazine. Don't ramble on and on — keep your writing concise and to the point. Make sure your examples and anecdotes help your article reach the goal you decided on at the beginning. And stick to the word count that the magazine specifies in its writer's guidelines — if your article is too short or too long, it probably won't be accepted for publication!

Good magazine articles have four parts:

- **The Lead.** The lead is another term for the first paragraph of the article. A good lead catches the attention of the reader and makes them want to keep reading. Good techniques for leads include using a quote, telling an anecdote, or presenting interesting facts. You might also tell a brief story about a particular person who serves as an example of your topic.

- **The Introductory Paragraph.** This paragraph comes immediately after the lead. It gives a capsule summary of what the entire article is going to be about. The purpose of this paragraph is to get the reader even more excited about reading the rest of your article!

- **The Body.** Here's where you get into the meat of your article. You want to present all of your facts and examples in a logical order that flows easily from one point to the next.

- **The Conclusion.** At the end of your article, you need one or two paragraphs to sum up the main points you've made. And here's another good place for a quote, an anecdote, or an interesting fact that will make a lasting impression on your reader!

Build A Niche

The way to get a reputation in the magazine industry is to write about the same subject, over and over. This is also exactly the strategy to use to maximize your income from writing magazine articles! Let me explain.

Say you write an article about gardening spades, like the article described in the sample letter above. You can take that same idea, give it a new twist, and sell it to other magazines as well! For example, you can do a feature article on the new all-steel spade for another publication. You can take any one of the other 19 spades you described and do the same thing. Or, for a completely different kind of magazine, you can do an article called "My First Spade," a nostalgia piece based on the spade your father gave you for your tenth birthday. Or you can do an article based on the spade of your great-grandfather, which has been passed down to you through three generations of your family.

You get the idea. Whether it's gardening spades, computers, cooking, or child care, write about what you know — over and over again! Before you know it, you'll be recognized as an authority in your field — and your mailbox will be bulging with checks! Which brings us to our next topic...

Getting Paid

Some magazines pay "on acceptance"; others pay "on publication." By all means, if you want to get paid faster, stick with magazines that pay "on acceptance." It could be six months or more before you see any money from a magazine that pays on publication; and even then, unforeseen delays could occur. Meanwhile, your article is spoken for and you don't have the chance to sell it to anyone else!

So, what can you expect to get paid? Rates vary wildly from magazine to magazine. When you're just starting out, you can expect to make anywhere from 5 cents to 25 cents a word. But soon, as you gain experience and have more clips to show, you can start commanding 50 cents to $2.50 a word! For a 1,000 word article (about four typed pages), that means you can make anywhere from $500 to $2,500! And that's just for a single article! As you can imagine, if you can write and sell an article every week or two, you'll really be in the money!

Sometimes magazines have standard rates they pay for small items that fit in their regular departments — say $50 to $100 per item. To find out the rates each magazine pays, see *Writer's Market*. Sometimes the writer's guidelines you sent for will have that information as well.

Don't Forget Trade Journals!

While your dream may be to have an article in *People, Life,* or *National Geographic*, don't forget about trade journals! These are magazines devoted to a particular trade or profession. They range from *Overdrive, The Magazine for the American Trucker,* to *Nailpro, The Magazine for Nail Professionals* (as in fingernails, that is!).

Now, the great thing about trade journals is that they pay just as much — and sometimes more! — than consumer magazines, PLUS they don't have the entire world of magazine writers knocking at their door. In other words, this is a perfect place where YOU can carve out a niche.

There is a great profile in *Writer's Market* of a freelancer who did just that. (See page 671 in the 1995 issue!) Briefly, this profile describes a woman who went to college in the Midwest and majored in dairy science. She eventually used her knowledge to break into the field of dairy industry publications. Now she writes for over 20 different periodicals. The editors at these publications know her and eagerly await her phone calls with her latest story ideas. And you can bet she's making a handsome living doing something that she absolutely loves to do!

Start Where You Are

This same kind of thing can happen to you. You don't need to go out and get any more education than you have right now. Instead, start from where you are. If you have a "regular job," what kind of trade journals are lying around your company's office? Have you ever picked them up and read them? If not, do so! You may find a trade journal you can write for right under your nose!

Likewise, if you went to school and got training in a specific area, look in *Writer's Market* for magazines under that subject heading. Then, attend the next trade show in your area for people in your business. Guess who comes to these trade shows? That's right, editors of the trade magazines YOU want to be published in!

Don't Delay, Begin Today!

So if magazine writing appeals to you, rest assured that there is a place for you in this huge and ever-expanding field! The market for consumer magazines is the best it's been in years. Nearly 800 new magazines were created in this country in 1994. And you can bet that all of them need writers—why not you? See Volume II for a starter list of consumer magazines and trade journals, and you'll be on the read to fame and fortune as a freelance writer for magazines!

204   Chapter 16: Writing for Magazines

Chapter 17: Homestead Publishing Program

Say you've written a book all your own. It might be a small book, 50 pages or less, on a subject that's your hobby or even your profession—whether it's beekeeping or bookkeeping, flower growing or computer research. Or, it might be a novel, a collection of short stories, or a book of poems. Maybe your book runs 100 pages, 200 pages, or even more!

The point is, whether your book is long or short, fiction or nonfiction, you have another option besides sending it around from publisher to publisher: you can publish your book yourself! Self-publishing has gained increasing acceptance in recent years. It used to be that self-publishing was frowned upon, or considered less worthy than having your book selected by a major publisher. But time is changing all that.

While there's no denying the prestige that goes along with a book contract, the fact of the matter is, those contracts are harder and harder to come by. Because more people are writing books than ever before, the odds of being signed by a major publisher have been drastically reduced. And you can end up waiting YEARS for it to happen!

The Story of *The Celestine Prophecy*

On the other hand, it's entirely possible for a self-published book to sell so many copies that major publishers <u>seek out</u> the authors and <u>offer</u> them contracts! One of the most recent examples of this phenomenon is *The Celestine Prophecy* by James Redfield. As of March 1995, this book stood at Number 1 on the New York Times best-seller list for fiction, and it has been on the best-seller list for over a year.

The Celestine Prophecy is currently available from Time Warner Books (and it's available on audiocassette as well)—but the author started out by publishing it himself. At first, people passed this book from hand to hand and told their friends about it. Before long the book became wildly popular, selling like hotcakes in small bookstores all over the country—and the world! Rumor has it that *The Celestine Prophecy* was the best-selling self-published book of all time! You can bet that the big publishing houses sat up and took notice.

And while the huge success of *The Celestine Prophecy* may be hard to duplicate, the facts are there: instead of waiting around, hoping and praying to be signed by a big publisher one day, many people are taking matters into their own hands and publishing their own books NOW. You can, too. And this chapter will show how you can do just that—with no more than the computer or typewriter you have at home, plus the help of your local copy shop!

The Homestead Publishing Program: A Summary

Here, then, are the main points of our Homestead Publishing Program:

- Create the final document just how you want it to look, using whatever "technology" you have at home right now—whether it's a typewriter or a computer.

- Start small. Use your local copy shop as a printer. Work with them closely to get the best book you can for the least money. Print small batches at first to give yourself a chance to perfect your product.

- Market your book around town at first. Hold booksigning parties, lectures by the author (you!) and other special events that will draw people together who want to buy your book.

- As your book takes off, graduate to more expensive printing methods and print more copies at a time. And congratulate yourself on your publishing success!

Now sit back while we take you through each of these steps in detail. By the end of this chapter, you'll have all the information you need to make the Homestead Publishing Program work for you!

The Desktop Publishing Revolution

No doubt you've heard about the desktop publishing revolution. A great many people, working from home with their own PCs or Macintosh computers, are churning out published materials at a mile a minute—including books!

If you already have your own computer at home, you can easily make the transition to being a self-publisher. All you need is the right desktop publishing program for your computer. For Macintosh users, the most popular program is Pagemaker; for PC users, it's Pagemaker for Windows. You can take classes in how to use these programs just about anywhere, from your local community college to adult education to special seminars that advertise all over the country. In a matter of weeks, you'll have all the skills you need to produce a professional-looking book.

But if you don't have these desktop publishing programs and don't want to buy them, don't despair! You can certainly use a word processing program like Microsoft Word, Word Perfect, Claris Works, or Wordstar to do a simple book layout. In fact, <u>whatever</u> program you usually use for typing purposes can be adapted to produce a book. I strongly recommend starting with the technology you have on hand and moving up from there.

One word of advice regarding dot matrix printers: dot matrix output is generally harder to read than output from a laser printer. I recommend taking your computer file to a copy shop or service bureau that will print out your file on a laser printer. It costs a little extra, but you will be much more pleased with the final results. OR, simply hand your computer disk to a copy shop that has a Docutech machine and let them take it from there! (See the section on the Docutech below.)

<u>Whatever you do, DON'T let the lack of money or equipment stand in your way—simply resolve to work with what you have!</u> Which brings me to the next subject . . .

What If You Don't Have A Computer?

My advice if you don't have a computer is, don't let that stop you, either! I've seen plenty of great self-published books that were banged out on a typewriter and run off at a local copy shop.

In fact, some of my favorite small poetry books were produced by a friend of mine using this exact method. He typed his poems on clean white sheets and had them made into booklets at the copy shop, with the pages folded in half and all stapled together in the middle. (Copy shops have folding and stapling machines that produce a very nice-looking product!)

For the front cover, he would use the enlarger button on the copy machine and make his typewriter type very large. For the back cover, he would use a photograph of himself with a brief biography.

My friend would use an attractive colored paper for the cover and plain white for the insides. These books were very professional-looking and cost him next to nothing—and he was able to sell them around town for $5 apiece, making a tidy profit!

Other friends of mine have made similar books and added special touches, like copying a black-and-white illustration onto the cover and then coloring it in by hand. Another decorative touch is to use rubber stamps and colored ink pads to decorate the cover of your book. Let your imagination run wild—you'll amaze yourself and be proud of the results!

Basic Rules for Book Production

- The front cover should always include the title and the author of the book (you!).

- The back cover should always include the ISBN number. (See the section on ISBN numbers later in this chapter.) The ISBN number must also appear somewhere in the first few pages of the book.

- A nice touch is to include a "title page" inside the book that repeats the title and author from the cover. See the very book you're holding for an example!

- In the front of the book, along with the ISBN number, put the word "Copyright," the copyright symbol, the year, and your name like this:

Copyright © 1995 by John Doe

Doing this gives you copyright protection according to the law. You don't have to pull any stunts like putting a book in the mail and sending it back to yourself. That's an old wives' tale of how to copyright your book. The line described above is sufficient.

- For extra protection, add the following statement to your book under the copyright line:

All rights reserved. No part of this book may be reproduced or utilized in any form or by any means, electronic or mechanical, including photocopying, recording, or by any information storage and retrieval system, without permission in writing from the author.

(Note: If you use these sentences, be sure to add your address so people can contact you if necessary. Use a post office box rather than a street address if at all possible.)

- Include a Table of Contents so people can find the chapters or sections of your book easily.

- Number all the pages, from start to finish.

- Add a "Dedication" or "Acknowledgments" page if you want to dedicate your book to someone, or thank the people who helped you prepare it.

- Leave generous margins on all of the pages. Doing so will make your book easier to read.

- If your book is a nonfiction book, consider adding an index. See the chapter on indexing for helpful hints! An index can make your book more useful by helping readers find whatever topic they're interested in.

Visit Your Copy Shop

Before you go any further with your self-publishing plans, pay a visit to your local copy shop. Tell them you want to produce a booklet or book and let them know approximately how many pages you expect it to be. Look at the kinds of paper they carry and think about the paper you'd like to use for the cover and inside pages of your book. Then select the paper you like and have the copy shop give you an estimate for copying, collating, and stapling your book together.

Of course, you must also tell the copy shop how many books you want. A rule of thumb is that the more copies you order, the cheaper the price is per book. On the other hand, it's far better to print fewer copies, sell them all, and use the profits to reprint, than to be worried about the huge stack of books that's gathering dust in a corner of your garage.

Here's my recommendation: print 100 books to start out if you can afford it; if money is tight, try for 50. Then test your market and see how sales go. When you sell out, you can reprint right away. Also, if it turns out you've made a mistake that you want to correct in your next printing, you'll be able to do so very soon—since you're bound to sell out within a few months' time!

If you're completely strapped for money, copy your books in batches of 10 and staple them together yourself. You'll soon see that having any book at all is better than none—and as you sell your batches of 10, you can make more copies each time. Keep plowing your profits back into producing more and better copies of your book, and you'll make your success even sweeter!

The Docutech

The latest development in copy shop technology is a wonderful machine called the Docutech. This machine makes copies better, faster, and cheaper than any conventional copy machine. What's the secret? The Docutech works from a <u>digital master.</u> In other words, it takes your original pages or computer disk and creates a computerized master file from them. This computerized file is used to print the copies.

Copies that come from a Docutech are many times sharper and cleaner than other kinds of copies. And this machine is so fast that it can print up all the copies you want of a book in less than half the time of a regular copier!

You might call around to some of the larger copy shops in your area to find out if they have a Docutech. Now, this is not a machine that you can operate yourself; you must leave your job at the copy shop and let trained employees do the work for you. So much the better! Believe me, the time and money you save with the Docutech makes it well worth the effort to try and find one in your area!

Saddle Stitching Vs. Perfect Binding

The <u>binding</u> of a book refers to how the left-hand side is held together. For small books, the most common way to do this is with staples. This is called saddle stitching. Saddle stitching is what's commonly used for books under 50 pages long that are made by folding sheets of 8 1/2 x 11 paper in half. (In other words, the finished book measures 5 1/2 x 8 1/2.)

But when a book like this gets to be more than 50 pages, it no longer lies flat when it's stapled together. That's when you need to start thinking about perfect binding. This is a method that uses glue, cloth tape, plastic strips, and other similar materials to hold the left-hand edge of the pages together.

Perfect binding is a good method to use for larger books, like books that measure a full 8 1/2 x 11 inches in size. Ask your copy shop to show you examples of the different binding materials they use. Then pick the one that appeals to you most and suits the kind of book you are making.

Cover Options

Your first thought may be, "I want a nice glossy cover with lots of color printing on it, just like the books I see in the bookstore!" This is a feeling I can understand and appreciate. Glossy covers ARE beautiful, and they look so pretty sitting on the shelf. But believe me, your wallet may not think this is such a good idea!

My advice is this: if it will set your mind at rest, go ahead and get a printing quote for a glossy cover with colored ink. If you can afford it, great! But if you're just starting out, I think you're better off saving your hard-earned cash for a glossy cover on the second or third printing.

Look at your first book as a trial run—as a concept that you will improve and refine over time. Don't blow your entire savings account getting a super-deluxe cover on a book that you may want to change over the next few months anyway! Give yourself the option of improving the book over the first few months of its life—don't shoot yourself in the foot by investing all you've got the first time around.

I'll let you in on a secret. The publisher of this book uses THIS VERY METHOD, to great success! Only a few months' worth of books are printed at any one time, so that subsequent editions can be corrected for errors or improved by adding new information. As a result, readers such as yourself are much happier with the product, and the publisher keeps costs under control.

The same principle applies if you've written a novel. For example, what can you do if you suddenly discover that you left out the last page of Chapter 7, or inserted (God forbid) the wrong version of Chapter 10 from your word processor? If you went to a big-time printer and got 1,000 books with glossy covers, believe me, you have no choice but to tear your hair out. On the other hand, if you printed 50 books with plain paper covers at your local copy shop, it's no sweat—you just insert a correction page for now, and make it right the next time around!

ISBN Numbers

These are the official-looking numbers that you find on the back cover and in the first few pages of any book that's for sale in a bookstore. If you want to sell your book in bookstores, it must have an ISBN number! (It stands for International Standard Book Number.)

Here's how you get one. Go to the reference desk at your local library and ask for the ISBN form. They will have it behind the counter. Make a copy of it, fill it out, and send it in—it's as easy as that! The supplier will send back 10 numbers to you—so you'll have extras on hand for your next book project. The cost is about $100. Now that's not cheap, but think of it this way—it comes out to about $10 per book if you do more than one title. (And over the years, you probably will—it's amazing how self-publishing grows on you!)

If you absolutely cannot afford the ISBN number, by all means, go ahead and print up your book anyway—just be aware that most bookstores will probably not be able to carry it. You can still sell copies to your friends and to others around town, and before long you'll sell enough to get the ISBN number for your second printing!

What About Bar Codes?

You'll notice that most books in the bookstore have a special "bar code" printed on the back cover. Though bookstores do prefer it, the bar code is still optional—but the ISBN number is not. When you're just starting out, simply get the ISBN number and make sure to print it on the back cover of your book and somewhere in the first few inside pages. There's no need to go through the trouble of getting the bar code as well.

What About Library of Congress Numbers?

Some books—though not all—have Library of Congress numbers in addition to ISBN numbers. They fall into the same category as the bar codes described above—nice, but not essential for your book. The Library of Congress number represents just another classification system, and more work for you. The really important one is the ISBN number—so if you're going to get official, put your money and effort towards the ISBN, and forget about the Library of Congress number.

What About Photographs and Artwork?

Photographs and artwork definitely add visual appeal to your book. They also add significantly to the cost of producing your book. When you're first starting out, keep photographs and artwork to a minimum—they just do not reproduce that well on conventional copy machines. "Line art," like simple black-and-white drawings, is usually OK.

Everything changes for the better, however, if you are using the mighty Docutech. The Docutech reproduces photos and artwork with amazing accuracy and clarity, and at amazingly cheap prices!

Pricing Your Book

How much should you charge for your book? That depends on how big it is and what it looks like. You might visit your bookstore and do some first-hand market research. What are other books in your category selling for these days?

No matter how small your book is—even if it's just a tiny booklet—try not to sell it for less than $5. Think about it this way: most books cost more than that, and it even costs more than that to go to the movies in most places (unless you hit the bargain shows, of course!)

Marketing Your Book

Here's the fun part: selling your book to everyone you know! You can really get creative figuring out ways to make a big splash with your "baby." Here are a few suggestions:

- By all means, have a booksigning party at a local bookstore. Make sure the event is advertised in the paper and print up flyers to post around town. At the event, read excerpts from the book and sell copies afterwards—which you sign to each person individually upon purchase! Then, make sure all the bookstores in town carry your book!

- Have as many additional booksigning parties as you can. If you belong to any clubs or community organizations, for example, have them put your booksigning on the agenda for an upcoming meeting—or make it a special event with all the trimmings! The more festive, the better! Serve refreshments afterwards, and then sell, sell, sell your book!

- Offer your services as a lecturer for various civic and community groups. Give a speech about your book, have a question and answer period, and then sell copies afterwards. If your book is a fiction book, speak at writing classes and seminars. If your book is a nonfiction book, speak to any group that might have an interest in your topic.

- Be sure your local newspaper and other community publications know about your book. Send them notices of any booksignings or lectures you do. Try to interest them in reviewing your book. You might send a sample copy of your book to local book reviewers.

- Attend book fairs, trade shows, even swap meets, and sell your book wherever you go. Always keep a box of books in your car—you never know who you'll run into around town! You get the idea—keep pushing, and your first edition will be sold out before you know it!

- Here's a final tip. Bookstores usually keep 40% of the book's selling price for themselves. So if you really want to make money, do it by selling your books on your own! Look at bookstore sales as a mere supplement to your main marketing strategy. Be creative and find ways to sell books on your own wherever you go!

The Sky's the Limit!

Once your book has taken off, there's no place to go but up! After you've sold out your first batch of books, print up a second batch with any changes or corrections you want. When you get to the third batch, you might want to start spending more money on production costs—adding some colored ink to the cover, for example.

From this point forward, print more copies of your book at one time, and make more improvements from time to time. Before long you may decide to spring for that glossy cover you wanted all along. And who knows—maybe you've produced the next *Celestine Prophecy*, and the New York publishers will be knocking on YOUR door. You'll never know unless you try it—and meanwhile, you'll be having the time of your life as a bona fide published author!

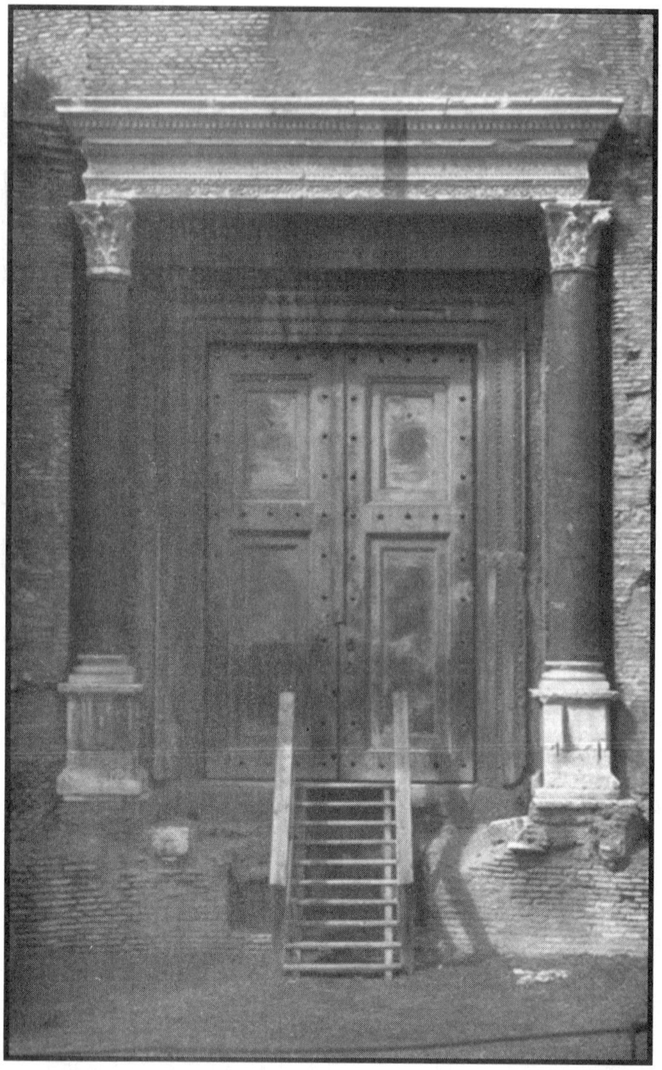

Chapter 18:
How to Read Critically

Just about everyone loves a "good read"—the feeling of being so absorbed in a book that you can't seem to put it down. But have you ever asked yourself why some books simply "work," and others just leave you cold? What's the secret behind the success of a page-turner versus a book you toss aside without even finishing the first chapter?

The answer to this question has to do with a book's plot and underlying structure. By developing the ability to evaluate a story and describe its structure, <u>you can turn your love of reading books into a valuable money-making skill!</u>

Learning to read critically has many, many benefits. You'll become a reader with a mind of your own — a reader who can't be fooled. You'll positively know what is true and what is "bunk" in any book. Plus, you'll be able to write better yourself, or help someone else write better. But most of all, you'll be able to make money by reading manuscripts for an editor or agent and telling them why the writing is good, or what is lacking in the piece.

The criteria for good writing are not as elusive as you might think. There's a lot of bunk out there, but there's also writing that could be good — if it were crafted better, or if it had a clear idea at the center of it. As a professional reader, you'll learn how to get straight to the heart of any problems in a book manuscript, describe those problems accurately, and make suggestions for improvements.

This chapter will deal with basic rules for judging a book's structure, and for evaluating the essence of a manuscript or already published work. First, we'll take a look at guidelines that apply primarily to fiction writing. Later in this chapter we'll present guidelines for analyzing nonfiction writing.

The Basics of Story Structure

When you're reading any type of fiction, from novels to short stories to plays, you can begin your evaluation by asking the following questions:

Does the manuscript start with a clear, interesting statement? Does it make you care? Are you hooked?

Virtually every book written about writing talks about the need for "the narrative hook." This is exactly what it sounds like. Readers are like fish, casually swimming along the streams of a bookstore's aisles. They may be attracted to a book by its cover, but what hooks them into reading the book — and what makes them plunk down money for it — is often the very first sentence.

"It was the best of times. It was the worst of times." So begins *A Tale of Two Cities*, the great classic by Charles Dickens. Nearly anyone would be intrigued enough to keep reading. It's an excellent example of a memorable first sentence — in fact, it's so memorable that even today people use it in everyday speech. You might have said those very words yourself without knowing where they come from!

A good first sentence is the key to a good first paragraph — and the first paragraph has a very important role to play as well. Read on!

Does the first paragraph give you an idea about the entire story?

Clearly, Charles Dickens revealed in one well-crafted statement what he plans to show us for the rest of *A Tale of Two Cities*: the best and worst of times. We need only finish the paragraph to see where we are and who we are supposed to be interested in and caring about.

Clear, declarative statements in the first paragraph pull the reader in and create the momentum to keep reading. In the first paragraph, it helps if we learn where the story is taking place and which character matters most in the story. Every story needs a central character — a character who matters even more than the scenery, and certainly more than the other characters.

Sometimes a play or book will start with a prologue. The purpose of a prologue is to set the stage or tone of the piece and prepare us for the action to come. An example of this can be found in Shakespeare's play *Macbeth*. The prologue contains the appearance of three weird sisters, or witches. They speak of war, and they speak of Macbeth and how they will meet him. The scene is spooky and foreboding. We are chilled by the witches and anticipate a dark tale. This is precisely the effect Shakespeare intended.

A story that doesn't begin swiftly, that doesn't know what it's about, and that isn't interested in entertaining or enlightening the reader, is simply not worth reading — and you can usually tell all of this from the very first paragraph!

Who are the main characters?

When reading any manuscript critically, you must decide whether the main characters are clearly present and in focus. Sometimes a writer makes the mistake of neglecting to focus on one or two special characters. This does serious damage to the narrative flow.

Generally speaking, a few characters in every story need to stand out clearly from the crowd. Most often, there is one main character, called the protagonist. This is the hero or leader of the cause — an old man who's trying to save his farm, a woman who goes to Africa to study great apes, a young lawyer searching for justice against all odds.

A good writer will zero in and identify the main character as soon as possible. And, the writer will make sure that this hero or heroine has the energy to carry us through the story. Now a hero, or heroine, can only have energy if they want something — which brings us to the next question:

What is the chief goal of the protagonist?

A protagonist without a goal can hardly be called a protagonist at all! Protagonists are categorized as sympathetic or pathetic, depending on the nature of their goals. A sympathetic protagonist, such as Romeo in *Romeo and Juliet*, wants something achievable, desirable, and visible. Romeo wants Juliet. His desire for her is something we all can understand, and something most of us dream of having — the kind of wondrous love and attraction that Romeo enjoys with Juliet. We can also imagine him having her for his wife. Therefore, his goal is visible.

A pathetic heroine is someone like Medea in the classic Greek story. She is a wronged woman, because her husband cheated on her. She murders their children to get back at him. In this act she also completely ruins herself. From the beginning, her goal is not visible or achievable in our minds. But at some level we can identify with her emotions. Even though she is a pathetic heroine, she is a compelling character whose story has lived for over two thousand years.

Shakespeare's Macbeth is another example of a pathetic protagonist. His goal is to achieve ultimate power in the kingdom of Scotland. He sets about to murder the king in order to achieve that goal. The only reason we keep watching, and don't turn away in disgust, is that somewhere deep inside ourselves we'd all like to be powerful. The story holds our attention for other reasons, too. Macbeth struggles with himself, with his own decision to carry out the murder. We can identify with this kind of indecision. The payoff comes when he suffers the consequences of his dastardly act.

All these are classic examples of protagonists who are truly drawn. They are true because their goals are clear and their emotions, and the choices they make based on those emotions, are understandable. In every story, it is absolutely necessary that we understand the main character — in other words, why they do what they do.

Fairy tales provide a good way to see motivation clearly. Jack of the story "Jack and the Beanstalk" must save his family from starvation. This is an understandable circumstance — we all get hungry! He trades the family cow for magic beans. We don't want him to do this, we can see the writing on the wall, but we understand why he does it. And because Jack is in need, we pull for him.

In the case of "Hansel and Gretel," we have two protagonists who represent the male and female sides that exist within all of us. Their goal to get back home is human, believable, and visible. Of course, they don't get there right away. That brings us to the next necessary element of a good story. Someone tries to stop them. In reading any story, you must ask yourself:

Who is the antagonist?

The hero, or hero and heroine, can have what they want, if only.... The "if" part of the story, the part where the hero has difficulty, is achieved by putting hurdles in his path. This could be quicksand at his feet, a snake in his bed, or best of all, another person whose whole reason for being is to stop the hero from achieving his goal. For example, in "Hansel and Gretel," a witch in an enchanted little cottage made of gingerbread. The witch is the antagonist. The antagonist is most interesting when he or she is really powerful — possibly even more powerful than the protagonist.

You could say that Macbeth is his own worst enemy. Certainly he keeps putting himself in harm's way. This is true of Indiana Jones as well. But both these heroes have flesh and blood enemies — and sometimes, lots of them. These enemies provide the hero with a way to become more of who he is, because when a person is challenged, the best and worst of their character is revealed.

Where is the conflict?

Some stories don't have villains or obvious threats to overcome. However, all good stories have conflict. In *Little Women*, Jo struggles to become a real writer, a published writer. Her first book is rejected by a publisher. Then a man she admires tells her she's writing drivel. She fights depression, the big city, homesickness, and when things couldn't get worse, her dear sister dies. But all of this pushes her to write from the heart — to write a really memorable book, and in doing so to find fulfillment.

If Jo had been published right away, we might not have believed it — and if we did, we wouldn't find her story very interesting. Jo would not have the opportunity to grow or change. *Little Women* would also have shrunk from a full-length novel to a very short story.

Does the action get more interesting?

There is a sign above my desk. It reads: "MAKE THINGS HARDER! Tension, ordeal, struggle, jeopardy." I know that unless my heroine has to struggle, she won't learn — more about herself, about life, about love. Unless my heroine has to fight for what she wants, the story will lack grit, honesty, and therefore, substance. This probably seems like the perfect recipe for a very depressing story. But on the contrary, every story — whether it's a comedy or a tragedy — must have conflict!

As long as there is something for the protagonist to fight for and fight against, there will be a feeling of movement in the story. In order for there to be a feeling of urgency and importance, circumstances must get more and more desperate, harder for the hero.

It also helps if the story has a goal or mission or desired result that must be accomplished in a limited time. This is called the "clock" of the story. Many modern movies have this time limit in place before the first half hour is over. In the movie "48 Hours," Eddie Murphy and Nick Nolte have exactly two days to accomplish their mission. In "Moonstruck," Cher and Nicholas Cage must get together and seal their love before his brother gets home. The characters don't know this, but the audience does. Either way, it increases the stakes, and therefore our involvement in the story.

Who is the love interest?

The sign on my desk that says "MAKE THINGS HARDER!" also says "HOPE." Many protagonists need a love interest to remind them that life is worth living. It has been said that in order to be happy people need only three things: someone to love, something to do, and something to look forward to.

In *Gone With the Wind*, Scarlett O'Hara focuses on Ashley, fulfilling the love interest part of her goal. Her desire for him keeps her going despite the trials and tribulations of war and loss. She never really gives up on the idea of having him for her own, until near the end. What is good for Scarlett is also good for the story. Scarlett's desire is like an engine with plenty of coal, driving her, the story, and the reader straight on to the finish.

Who is the mirror?

Depth can be added to a story through a character who mirrors the protagonist. In *Gone with the Wind*, Scarlett is mirrored by Melanie. Melanie is so good and so true. Her struggles mirror Scarlett's in that she goes through similar trials, experiences the same types of loss, but her reaction is gracious where Scarlett's reaction is cynical. Melanie is everything that Scarlett is not. She's what Scarlett could be, if only Scarlett were more open to what life is all about.

Sometimes writers get confused and try to make the mirror the same character as the love interest, or make the antagonist the same character as the mirror. But the antagonist is not the love interest. The mirror is not the love interest…or any other combination. If the functions of the characters are kept clean and clear, the story will unfold much more easily and satisfactorily.

Try this test: take any novel or play you're reading at the moment and ask yourself if you can clearly identify the protagonist, antagonist, mirror, and love interest.

What is the theme?

So many stories, and so many plays, are written without the author paying any attention to the underlying theme. This happens with professional writers as well as beginners. My friend Beth, a playwright, says she always takes lots of notes, writes several basic outlines, and imagines the beginning scene of her plays before she identifies the theme. She says, "Before I get too far in, I need to know the theme. It helps if I'm asking myself from the start, what is this about?"

Beth tells the following story from her own personal experience of writing plays: "When I was writing a musical drama about Joan of Arc, I thought, it could be about female oppression. It could be about the horror of politics, or it could be about fear of someone different."

"After reading everything I could find on the subject, I began to outline the basic action of the piece. It was then I realized that what interested me most was that such an unlikely person would be asked to do such extraordinary things. Imagine, a girl told by angels to go to a fearful, uncrowned king, convince him to give her an army, drive the English out of France, and then take the monarch to be crowned."

"At the time I was going to Hollywood meetings with studio and network heads, trying to get them to buy my stories, and subsequently give me an army to film them. I couldn't believe the amount of struggle I faced in screwing up my courage to approach these powerful people, and the kind of vision it required to go forward with confidence. I prayed a lot. Joan of Arc seemed like a person who was the ultimate symbol for that kind of activity. So, I thought this story is really about vision and courage. Once I decided that was my theme, the important and necessary scenes I needed to tell my story began to reveal themselves to me."

A clearly defined theme keeps the writing on track. When you sit down to read a work critically, it may not be obvious at first what the theme is. Most writers don't announce it. But by the time you've finished the first quarter of the piece, whether it's a novel, short story, or play, you should be able to make a good guess as to what it's all about underneath the action.

Here's another example: on the surface "Phantom of the Opera" is about a burned guy who strives to win the affection of a beautiful woman. Underneath that plot the theme is: self acceptance and love.

What is the premise?

A premise is not the plot or the theme. A premise is the idea behind the story; the philosophical point of view that the writer keeps in his mind as he's writing. The premise of *Macbeth* is "obsession with power leads to destruction." The premise of *Gone with the Wind* is "selfishness leads to loss of love." The premise of *Little Women* is "love makes life worth living."

A clear premise enables the writer to stay focused on the action of the story. If you are reading a manuscript and your attention wanders, or you like the characters but it isn't clear why they're doing what they're doing, the fault may lie with the absence of a premise.

If you're writing a story, you can find the premise by asking yourself, "What do I really believe?" Maybe your life experience has shown you that if you try very hard to achieve a goal, such as winning a promotion, you can achieve it if you're clever and energetic. So, in writing a story about a knight in the twelfth century, you may find that using the premise "cleverness and energy leads to winning" is a true statement that can be explored through your hero. It's a statement that will inform your story — and it will make your story deeper and truer, because it reflects your very own belief.

What is the catalytic event?

Every story needs energy to get it off the ground. Some event must be presented that forces the characters to do something. This event is the catalyst for the action of the story. It may not occur right away, but it should happen as soon as possible. Usually, the ordinary world of the main character is shown first, and then that world suddenly changes.

In John Grisham's novel *The Firm*, a young couple celebrates the husband's (Mitch's) graduation from college. Right in this first scene, Mitch announces that he's got a job offer — the sweetest deal any graduate could ever dream of. Suddenly the couple is plunged into a new world, tainted slightly by their suspicion that if it sounds this great, it can't be real. They must deal with things they've never dealt with before. They have to make decisions. Now that's enough energy to get the story really moving and to make the characters react. This catalyst, this explosion in their lives, makes the book a real page-turner.

Does the action of the story lead to a climax of events?

All stories need a climax. This is an event near the end of the story where all the efforts of the protagonist and all the efforts of the antagonist come together in a dramatic clash. In a western, this is the gunfight they've all been preparing for. In *Hamlet*, the climax of the play is the last court scene where everyone gets killed. In "Hansel and Gretel," the climactic scene is when they shove the witch in the oven.

Are the details interesting enough to keep you reading?

The way in which a writer describes a character, or an event — the kind of language used and the pictures conjured up in the reader's mind — makes the difference between a tolerable reading experience and a memorable one. When Dylan Thomas in "Under Milkwood" describes the Welsh sea as being Bible-black, or tells us that the nun's sleeve unfurled like a pirate flag, we get a definite picture and an odd mixture of feeling — both giddy and foreboding — from his description. It is this ability to paint with words, more than any other single thing, that inspires critics and readers alike to find pleasure in reading.

Detail is also necessary in character development. If even a simple schoolteacher in a story has an interesting past, an intellectual life, and a philosophy all her own, that character will hold our attention and even intrigue us. Jean Brody in *The Prime of Miss Jean Brody* is a character who captivates us from the first page. Her mission of turning girls onto the passion of life would not be nearly so compelling to read if she weren't eccentric.

How to Apply These Rules of Structure

Generally speaking, the rules of structure described above can apply to all forms of fiction writing, including children's books, plays, screenplays, and to some degree, even poetry.

Here's an example from the world of children's books. Imagine Beatrix Potter's Peter Rabbit without a problem — there wouldn't be much of a story! Peter, the protagonist, spies the new vegetables coming up in Mr. McGregor's garden (the catalytic event). He wants fresh vegetables to eat (the visible, desirable, achievable goal). Mr. McGregor, the antagonist, wants to rid himself of the pest of a rabbit (the conflict). Peter's mother, the mirror, goes about procuring food in the proper way. There's no love interest here, but that doesn't make it any less of a good story. Peter has hope and he's clever, even as he's constantly getting himself into tense, stressful, life-threatening ordeals. The theme is foolish ambition. The premise is "uncontrollable appetites lead to pain."

Naturally, the rules for structure are broken frequently. In the right hands, the story won't suffer. The recent movie "Pulp Fiction" comes to mind. The writer/director chose to tell the story by focusing on several individuals. He also elected a nonlinear type of structure. Nevertheless, the seemingly separate stories interweave in relationship to each other, and the tension builds — all under the obvious theme of violence. Every other scene builds the sense of chaos and jeopardy for the John Travolta character, and we are made to fear for everyone surrounding him. When Travolta isn't in jeopardy, the Bruce Willis character is. Antagonists for these characters are everywhere, behind every door. It should be noticed as well that each scene gets more and more tense until the climactic scene in the restaurant where, in this circle of violence, we come back to where we started.

Practice What You've Learned!

Begin learning to read critically by analyzing a favorite short story or a recent novel you liked. See if you can identify the theme, the premise, the catalytic event, the protagonist and his or her goals. Write down the areas of conflict. Identify the antagonist and the love interest, if there is one. When you go to a movie or a play, think about what you've seen later. Analyze why the movie worked, or if it fell flat, ask yourself the above questions until you can state clearly what would have made the movie better.

Reading Nonfiction Critically

The term nonfiction refers to factual writings such as books, informational articles, reviews, opinions, essays and reports. In learning to read nonfiction critically, you'll find that many of the rules for fiction apply here as well — such as the necessity for theme and conflict. However, there are different ways to ask the right questions when analyzing nonfiction.

What is this manuscript about?

The time-tested rule is that informative writing should contain the following: Thesis, Antithesis, Synthesis. That means that the problem or primary subject (thesis) is stated clearly and forthrightly. This is followed closely by what is in the way of solving the problem (antithesis). The article concludes with the synthesis — or, how the thesis and antithesis are resolved.

The first step in writing any nonfiction piece is to make a declarative sentence. If I were to write about AIDS in children, I would most likely begin: "The AIDS epidemic in America is a plague which has taken the lives of over 20,000 children." I would prove this statement by identifying a factual study. Then I would tell how many kids are suffering with the disease who are waiting for a cure.

I could elaborate on that sentence by comparing this disease to other socially frightening diseases in the past. Then I might write: "Often these children are treated badly in social situations. There is even evidence that a cure has been so long in coming because some elements in our society see the disease as just payment for past sins. Others believe it is a gay disease."

These statements form an antithesis because they state the obstacles to understanding and curing AIDS.

Now I have a thesis, and I have an antithesis. My article will try to bring these two elements together so that I end with a synthesis. If I know why I am writing the article in the first place, my job is much easier. To teach and to delight are really the only reasons to write anything. The goal of this piece on AIDS in children would be for me to teach: to combat ignorance about this dreaded disease by writing an educational and informative article.

What is the point of view of the writer?

Nonfiction is served best when the writer makes the point of view obvious. The trick is to not be pushy, or preachy. If I read a book in order to write a book review about it, I'm obviously going to have an opinion. The best review will show the readers why I liked the book. The key word here is SHOW. Anybody can make a statement. Whether or not that statement is believed by the reader is based on the authority commanded by the writer.

Authority is recognized or given to a writer in one of three ways:

- The writer has a bona fide reputation for knowing the facts, such as a heart surgeon who has performed many heart surgeries and writes an article dealing with his field of expertise.

- The writer has a working knowledge of the subject matter, such as a book reviewer who has read many books by the same author or on the same topic and makes an informed judgment about any new material that comes out.

- The writer has done adequate research so that the details are true and the sources for statements are based on fact. A case in point is an article dealing with the nuclear waste cover-up in Colorado which recently appeared in the LA *Times Magazine*. The article was believable because the writer interviewed grand jury members, studied transcripts, and revealed details of government studies and statistics.

When you read nonfiction, see if you can easily identify the point of view of the writer. Does the writer have authority in your eyes? Why or why not? Does the writer say anything specific that inspires your confidence, or destroys it? Answering questions like these will hone your skills as a critical reader.

Is the writing interesting?

Not every nonfiction book, essay, review, or article is going to appeal to everyone. But there are ways to determine if the subject is being treated in such a way as to inspire readers who already know something about the subject at hand.

The writing in any nonfiction work should be clear, brief, detailed, informed, and honest. In other words, the article should state its purpose; it should tell what needs to be told as economically as possible; and finally, details and anecdotes should be added to illuminate the subject further. Hopefully, the writing will be a fresh approach to the subject, something new. The reader should not come away feeling that the writer has a hidden agenda; the writer must tell the truth as he sees it and for the purpose stated at the beginning of the piece.

My playwriting friend Beth's first journalistic assignment was to write a theatre review on a production of Tom Stoppard's famous play, "Rosencrantz & Gildenstern Are Dead," for a community "throw-away" newspaper. She says, "For some reason they were still interested in me even after I misspelled Shakespeare throughout the article, and despite the fact that I wrote in a kind of distanced, academic way."

She adds, "Soon after I turned in the review, the editors took me to lunch and asked me what was going on. I explained that I was afraid that my English professor would see the review, and I wanted him to think that I could write about a play in a educated manner. They laughed and told me to tell it like I saw it, and when I didn't know something (like how to spell Shakespeare, or the content of Tom Stoppard's other plays) to either look it up or avoid mentioning it."

After that Beth had a lot more fun writing reviews, and eventually her writing became increasingly more informed and insightful. She sums up, "I found it takes a lot more energy to be pretentious than to just be yourself, and usually you don't fool anybody."

The bottom line for judging any nonfiction writing is whether the writer knows their subject, and cares enough to want to tell someone else about it in a way that is fresh, informative, and understandable.

Practice, Practice, Practice!

When you pick up the newspaper, go to the movies, or read a bedtime story to your children, try applying the guidelines we've talked about in this chapter. Think about the story at hand and how it is told. Analyze what you liked and didn't like about the movie, play, book, story, article, or review. Be sure to come up with very specific reasons for your opinions. You'll be developing your skills as a critical reader—skills that you can put to good use making money by reading books, as described in the rest of this one!

Chapter 19:
Self-Confidence is the Key

By now this book has done its job. You've been initiated into the fascinating world of reading books for pay. You have more know-how about making money in this field than most people accumulate in an entire lifetime. You've got all the background it takes to be a winner—to make $35,000 a year, or even more, reading books for pay!

Now it's time to put all this know-how to work for you. I know it's not easy to start something new—to begin a whole new line of work. At first you might feel uncertain about how to proceed, or you might even think to yourself, "I don't know how to do this. It's too hard for me."

Well, I'm here to tell you that YOU <u>CAN</u> DO IT! While it's natural to have doubts at first, you have everything it takes to overcome those doubts and to make a success out of reading books for pay. You just have to take that big leap of faith and BELIEVE IN YOURSELF.

This chapter will remind you just how qualified you are to read books for pay, and give you some tips that will do wonders to boost your confidence. Whenever you feel a hint of doubt creeping in, just refer to this chapter for the encouragement you need to "keep on keeping on!"

The Reading Habit: Your #1 Asset

When I first started reading books for pay, I was probably a lot like you. I didn't have a college degree—all I had was my love of reading, and the determination to succeed in doing something new, in a field where I knew no one and had no contacts.

The one thing I did have going for me was my love of books and reading. I had always read everything I could get my hands on. Even as a kid, I always had my nose in a book. I read biographies, fairy tales, short stories, novels, anything and everything!

This reading habit carried on into my adult years. Without even realizing it, I had developed a "feel" for what makes a good book. If you love reading, chances are that you have that same inner knack for telling what's right and what's wrong about a book. And that's the first thing you need to break into the field of reading books for pay!

Whenever your confidence starts to fail you, just remember that you have something to offer that many other people don't—and that's the sum total of all the years you've spent reading. No one can duplicate your experience in this area. You've already got an edge over the competition!

If you've read extensively in just one area—for example, romance novels or westerns—that's even better! You probably qualify as an expert in that area, and you'll have even more opportunities that you can apply specifically to that kind of book. So congratulate yourself, and know that you next best asset is free, too, and one that's just waiting for you to put it to good use . . .

Word of Mouth: Your Next Best Asset

If you give them a little push, people will hear about you through the grapevine. You just won't understand the magic of word of mouth until you try it!

When I first started out reading books for pay, I did whatever kind of work came my way. I let my family and friends know what I was up to, of course, not really thinking that I'd find work from the people I knew already. But was I ever surprised! Soon I found that some amazing opportunities just fell into my lap!

For example, a friend of mine asked me to read his short stories. I helped him revise his writing to make it sound better. He told other people about how I helped him, and then I got phone calls from those folks looking for the same kind of help! And whereas I didn't charge my friend money for helping him with his stories, the other people who called asked what I charged. They actually WANTED to pay me for my services!

To me, that was a miracle. But you'll find the same thing happening to you as you get started reading books for pay. Let people know what you're doing, and don't hesitate to do a favor for a friend. Every little favor you do at the beginning is planting the seeds for more work to come your way later. So plant your garden well, and you'll reap a bountiful harvest of work—more than you ever dreamed of!

Get a Business Card

If you're just getting started in reading books for pay, you can give your self-confidence a big boost by getting a business card. You can get business cards printed at your local copy shop for between $20-$30 for 500 cards. I think it's one of the best investments you make in yourself. Why?

You just won't believe the thrill that comes from having your name, your new profession, and your phone number on a business card. Somehow, it makes what you're doing seem more real—it's not just an idea anymore, or something you're thinking about doing but haven't actually done yet.

Pick out the field you want to specialize in, and put that on your business card. Your card might say, "Mary Jones, Proofreader" and then your phone number. Or you could say, "Copyeditor," "Indexer," "Audio Book Reader," or any one of the other professions we talk about in this book. Put your address, too, if you know you'll be in one place for awhile. A post office box is especially good for this purpose.

Hand out your business cards wherever you go. Tack them up in laundromats or at your local copy shop. Put them wherever you see those business card bulletin boards around town. Soon the phone will start ringing—you'll discover people and opportunities right in your own town that you never knew existed!

Use Your Cards When Approaching Publishers—
And Think About Letterhead

The other thing you can do is enclose a business card along with each letter you write to a publisher, based on the sample letters included in this book. Now that will definitely make you stand out in the crowd, and add a degree of professionalism you just wouldn't have otherwise. If you really want to go the extra mile, get a simple letterhead printed up with your name on it. That combination will send your confidence level soaring when you approach publishers about getting work!

It's very true that in approaching publishers, you can't be too professional. I know from first-hand experience that having a business card and letterhead helped me get work reading books for pay. It just makes sense that if you show you care enough to present yourself well, you'll get noticed—and get the job!

When The Going Gets Tough, Don't Give Up

Many years ago, I moved across the country with my husband. While he had contacts for work in the new city that was our home, I didn't know a soul. At first I felt very discouraged. How was I going to find work?

What I did was, I went straight to the phone book and looked up all the publishers in the city—book publishers, magazines, newspapers, even publishers of directories. Then I wrote them all and called them to follow up, just like we describe in this book. And within two months, I ended up working freelance for two book publishers and a weekly entertainment newspaper.

Now, people who had been in that town for years couldn't believe that I got these jobs. What was my secret? It was simply showing up, really wanting to get the work, and being available to start at a moment's notice. I had the flexibility that the publishers needed, and so I was able to fit in with their schedules—which can sometimes be unpredictable at best.

You'll also notice that I didn't find a job overnight. In fact, I had contacted many, many publishers before I finally found the ones that would hire me. You may find the same is true when you approach publishers about reading books for pay. If you hear one or two "no's" and then give up, you'll be selling yourself short! You might have to make ten or even twenty phone calls before you get a nibble on the line.

The secret of your success is bouncing back after you hear the words, "Sorry, we don't have anything for you." Let those words spur you on to write the next letter or make the next phone call. Never waver in your determination that there's work out there for you, and you <u>will</u> find it!

If You Don't Ask, You Don't Get

Remember the old adage—If you don't ask, you don't get. If you just think to yourself, Gee, it would be nice to write book reviews for the local newspaper, but then never contact the newspaper about it, your career reading books for pay will never get off the ground. On the other hand, if you build up your courage and your resolve, and you actually make the initial contact, you'll have taken a giant leap towards your goal!

You see, even if you encounter rejection your first time out, you'll at least have gotten your feet wet. You'll gain experience in approaching publishers so that each letter you write and each phone call you make gets easier and easier. Soon you won't feel any nervousness at all! And you'll find that the more you practice approaching publishers, the better reception you'll get. Before too long, you'll be going in to meet the publishers in person—and not long after that, you'll be making the first deposits into your bank account from your efforts!

Don't Forget to Congratulate Yourself!

Make no mistake about it, you deserve lots of praise for simply buying this book! So few people really take action on any dream at all, whether it's reading books for pay or what have you.

You bought this book for a reason. You KNOW you have talent. Now it's just a matter of letting the world in on your secret. The saying, "Don't hide your light under a bushel" definitely applies here. There's plenty of work just waiting for people with ability and initiative like you. And if you don't get that work, somebody else will. So get out there and go for it—you'll wonder why you didn't start sooner!

Conclusion

Now you're ready to set off on your adventure of reading books for pay. All the information you need to get started is right here in this book. If you add a little persistence, you'll be sure to succeed!

But Wait—There's More!

Don't forget to use the material in Volume II to contact book publishers, children's book publishers, and magazine publishers about work opportunities. Each appendix has specific instructions about what to do, along with which chapter to refer back to for even more information.

Then, turn to the appendices on Writer's Conferences and Writer's Organizations. Here you'll find listings of groups that can help you learn even more about reading books for pay. They can even help you improve your skills in whatever area you're interested in.

The Glossary is always waiting if you need help with a particular term or phrase. And if you want to learn even more about reading books for pay, you'll find the sources in the Bibliography to be of great interest!

Let Us Hear From You!

We are always seeking to improve the quality of the information included in this volume. If you have suggestions, comments, or success stories to share with us, let us hear from you! Simply send to: Success Stories, Clarendon House, Inc., 1919 State St., Suite 112, Santa Barbara, CA 93101, Attention Rebecca Harris. To show you our appreciation, we'll send you a FREE publication that will be of GREAT INTEREST to you!

Appendix A: Writer's Conferences and Workshops

Attending a writer's conference or workshop can really jump start your career in reading books for pay. Whether you are a writer yourself — or whether you want to work for writers as a proofreader, copyeditor, indexer, or any one of the other professions described in this book — there's no better place to meet writers and learn the trade than one of these gatherings!

Scan this list for conferences and workshops that you would like to attend. Then, send each one a brief letter requesting conference dates and more information. Enclose a self-addressed, stamped envelope. Soon you'll be on your way to the conference of your choice — where you'll be sure to find money-making opportunities that you never dreamed existed!

(And remember, this list only scratches the surface of the hundreds of conferences and workshops available. Ask for *Literary Market Place* at the reference desk of your local library and consult the section called "Book Trade Workshops" for even more listings!)

"A Vision for Your Voice"
North Carolina Writers Network
Box 954
Carrboro, NC 27510

AMWA Workshops
American Medical Writers Association
9650 Rockville Pike
Bethesda, MD 20814-3998

Annual July Workshop Council of Authors and Journalists, Inc.
Box 830008
Stone Mountain, GA 30083-0001

Annual Writer's Conference

Northeast Texas Community College
Continuing Education
Box 1307
Mount Pleasant, TX 75455

Annual Writer's Seminar
The Society of Southwestern Authors (SSA)

Appendix A: Writer's Conferences and Workshops

Box 30355
Tucson, AZ 85751-0355

Arizona Authors' Association (AAA)
3509 E. Shea Blvd., Ste. 117
Phoenix, AZ 85018-1236

Arkansas Writers' Conference
Pioneer Branch of National League of American Pen Women
1115 Gillette Dr.
Little Rock, AR 72207

Aspen Writers' Conference
Box 5840
Snowmass Village, CO 81615

Austin Writers League
1501 West Fifth St., Ste. E2
Austin, TX 78703

Bay Area Writers Workshop
Box 620327
Woodside, CA 94062-0327

Bennington Writing Workshops
Bennington College
Bennington, VT 05201

Bread Loaf Writers' Conference
Middlebury College
Middlebury, VT 05753

The Brockport Writers' Forum
SUNY College at Brockport
c/o Dept. of English
Brockport, NY 14420

Brooklyn Writers Club
Box 184
Bath Beach Station
Brooklyn, NY 11214

Children's Book Writing and Illustration Workshops
Robert Quackenbush Studios
460 East 79th St.
New York, NY 10021

Clarion Workshop in Science Fiction and Fantasy Writing
Michigan State University
Lyman Briggs School
E-28 Holmes Hall
East Lansing, MI 48825-1107

Creative Communications Writing Conferences
Creative Communications
Box 2201
La Jolla, CA 92038

Deaf Playwrights Conference
National Theatre of the Deaf
5 W. Main St.
Chester, CT 06412

Deep South Writers Conference
University of Southwestern Louisiana
USL Box 44691
Lafayette, LA 70504

Eastern Writers' Conference
Salem State College
Graduate and Continuing Education
Salem, MA 01970

Festival of Poetry
The Robert Frost Place
Franconia, NH 03580

Florida Studio Theatre
1241 N. Palm Ave.
Sarasota, FL 34236
• Produces and develops new works by emerging playwrights.

Florida Suncoast Writers' Conference
University of South Florida
Department of English
Tampa, FL 33620

Paul Gillette's Writing Workshop
3284 Barham Blvd.,

Appendix A: Writer's Conferences and Workshops

Ste. 201
Los Angeles, CA
90068-1454

Green Lake Christian Writer's Conference
American Baptist Assembly
Green Lake, WI 54941-9599

Haystack Writing Program
Portland State University
Summer and Extended Programs
Box 1391
Portland, OR 97207

Heart of America Writers' Conference
Johnson County Community College
12345 College Blvd.
Overland Park, KS 66210

Annual Highland Summer Conference
Box 6935
Radford University
Radford, VA 24142

The Highlights Foundation Writers Workshop at Chautauqua
Highlights for Children, Inc.
711 Court St.
Honesdale, PA 18431

International Black Writers Conference
Box 1030
Chicago, IL 60690

Iowa Summer Writing Festival
116 International Center
Iowa City, IA 52242

Key West Literary Seminar, Inc.
419 Petronia St.
Key West, FL 33040

League of Vermont Writers
Box 1058
Waitsfield, VT 05673

Ligonier Valley Writers Conference
RD 4 Box 8
Ligonier, PA 15658

Francis Marion Writers' Retreat
Office of Continuing Education
Francis Marion College
Florence, SC 29501

Martha's Vineyard Writers' Workshops
The Nathan Mayhew Seminars of Martha's Vineyard, Inc.
Box 1125
Vineyard Haven, MA 02568

Mastering the Media Workshops
Desmond Communications
Box 30153
Santa Barbara, CA 93130

Midland Writers' Conference
Grace A. Dow Memorial Library
1710 W. St. Andrews
Midland, MI 48640

Midnight Sun Writers' Conference
University of Alaska-Fairbanks
English Department
Fairbanks, AK 99775

Midwest Writers Conference
Kent State University-Stark Campus
6000 Frank Ave. NW
Canton, OH 44720-7599

Mississippi River Writing Workshop
St. Cloud State University
English Department
720 Fourth Ave. S
Riverview 106
St. Cloud, MN 56301

Napa Valley Writers' Conference-Poetry and Fiction Sessions

Napa Valley College
2277 Napa-Vallejo Highway
Napa, CA 94558

Nebraska Writers Guild
14824 Parker Plaza
Omaha, NE 68154

New York State Writers Institute
State University of New York at Albany
1400 Washington Ave.
Albany, NY 12222

Newport Writers Conference
Box 12
Newport, RI 02840

"Of Dark and Stormy Nights"
Mystery Writers of America, Midwest Chapter
43 White Oak Circle
St. Charles, IL 61074

Outdoor Writers Association of America Conference
2017 Cato Ave., Suite 101
State College, PA 16801-2768

Ozark Creative Writers Inc. 20th Annual Conference
6817 Gingerbread Lane
Little Rock, AR 72204

Pacific Northwest Writers Conference
2033 Sixth Ave., #804
Seattle, WA 98121

Philadelphia Writers' Conference
Box 7171
Philadelphia, PA 19117

Port Townsed Writer's Conference
Centrum Foundation
Box 1158
Port Townsend, WA 98368

Robert McKee's Story Structure
Two Arts Inc.
12021 Wilshire Blvd., #868
Los Angeles, CA 90025

Romance Writers of America National Conference
Romance Writers of America
13700 Veterans Memorial Dr., Ste. 315
Houston, TX 77014

San Diego County Writers' Guild Christian Writing Seminar
Box 1171
El Cajon, CA 92022

San Diego State Writer's Conference
College of Extended Studies
San Diego State University
San Diego, CA 92182

Sandhills Writers' Conference
Augusta College
Continuing Education
2500 Walton Way
Augusta, GA 30910

Santa Barbara Writers Conference
PO Box 304
Carpinteria, CA 93014

Selling to Hollywood
Writers Connection
275 Saratoga Ave., Suite 103
Santa Clara, CA 95050

Shooting Star Writers Conference
Shooting Star Productions
7123 Race St.
Pittsburgh, PA 15208-1424

Short Course on Professional Writing
School of Journalism
University of Oklahoma
860 Van Vleet Oval
Norman, OK 73019

Appendix A: Writer's Conferences and Workshops

Society of Children's Book Writers, NW Oregon Retreat
22736 Vanowen St., Suite 106
West Hills, CA 91307

Southwest Florida Writers Conference
Edison Community College Continuing Education
809977 College Parkway SW
Fort Myers, FL 33906-6210

Southwest Writers Workshop
1336 Wyoming Blvd. NE, Suite C
Albuquerque, NM 87112-5000

Split Rock Arts Program
University of Minnesota
306 Westbrook Hall
77 Pleasant St. SE
Minneapolis, MN 55455

Squaw Valley Community of Writers Workshops
Squaw Valley Creative Arts Society
Box 2352
Olympic Valley, CA 96146

State of Maine Writers' Conference
Box 296
16 Colby Ave.
Ocean Park, ME 04063

Annual Skyline Writers' Conference
Skyline Writers' Club of North Royalton, Ohio
11770 Maple Ridge Dr.
North Royalton, OH 44133

Trenton State College Writers' Conference
Trenton State College
English Dept.
Hillwood Lakes CN4700
Trenton, NJ 08650

Mark Twain Writers Conference
Writers Conference
Hannibal-LaGrange College
Hannibal, MO 63401

UCI Extension Writers' Program
University of California, Irvine Extension
Box 6050
Irvine, CA 92716

The University of Kentucky Women Writers Conference
208 Patterson Office Tower
University of Kentucky
Lexington, KY 40506-0027

Wesleyan Writers Conference
Wesleyan University
Middletown, CT 06459

Willamette Writers' Conference
9045 SW Barbur Blvd., Suite 5A
Portland, OR 97219

Wisconsin Retreat
Society of Children's Book Writers and Illustrators
26 Lancaster Court
Madison, WI 53719-1433

Women's National Book Association, Los Angeles Chapter
Box 807
Burbank, CA 91503-0807

Writers Retreat
404 Crestmont Ave.
Hattiesburg, MS 39401

Writers Workshop in Children's Literature
Society of Children's Book Writers, Florida Chapter
2000 Springdale Blvd., Apt. F-103
Palm Springs, FL 33461

Writers Workshop in Science Fiction
University of Kansas
English Department

Lawrence, KS 66045

The Writing Center
601 Palisade Ave.
Englewood Cliffs, NJ
07632

Writing Today
Birmingham-Southern
College
Box A-3
Birmingham, AL 35254

Writing Workshop for People Over 57
Donovan Scholars
Program
University of Kentucky
Ligon House
Lexington, KY
40506-0442

Writing Workshops
University Extension
Unviersity of California
Davis, CA 95616

Yellow Bay Writers' Workshop
University of Montana
Center for Continuing
Education
Missoula, MT 59812

Appendix B: Writer's Organizations

Whether you're a writer or a freelancer in the publishing world who deals with writers on a regular basis, there is probably at least one professional organization on this list that can benefit you.

These organizations provide writers and like-minded individuals with many educational, business, and legal services. They publish newsletters, sponsor workshops and seminars, and some even provide health and life insurance coverage.

Some of these groups are only open to writers who meet certain professional criteria. When in doubt, ask! Some organizations, like the Society of Children's Book Writers and Illustrators, have two levels of membership: associate membership for new writers, and full membership for established writers.

To obtain more information from these groups, simply send a letter requesting a membership application and a brochure about the organization. Enclose a self-addressed, stamped envelope.

American Alliance for Theatre & Education
Theatre Dept.
Arizona State University
Tempe, AZ 85287
(Resources for aspiring playwrights)

American Book Producers Association
160 Fifth Ave., Suite 604
New York, NY 10010

American Medical Writers Association
9650 Rockville Pike
Bethesda, MD 20814

American Society of Journalists and

Authors, Inc.
1501 Broadway, Suite 302
New York, NY 10036

American Translators Association
1735 Jefferson Davis Hwy., Suite 903
Arlington, VA 22202

Appendix B: Writers Organizations

Arizona Authors Association
3509 E. Shea Blvd. #117
Phoenix, AZ 85028

Associated Writing Programs
Old Dominion University
Norfolk, VA 23529

Association of Authors Representatives
10 Astor Pl., 3rd Floor
New York, NY 10003

Association of Desktop Publishers
4677 30th St., Suite 800
San Diego, CA 92116

The Authors Guild
330 W. 42nd St., 29th Flr.
New York, NY 10036
(Specializes in helping authors with business and legal matters)

Children's Reading Round Table of Chicago
3930 N. Pine Grove #1507
Chicago, IL 60613
(Membership open to anyone interested in children's books)

Christian Writers Guild
260 Fern Lane
Hume Lake, CA 93628
(Sponsors a three-year correspondence course for editors)

Copywriters Council of America, Freelance
7 Putter Lane
Linick Bldg. 102
Middle Island, NY 11953

Council of Authors & Journalists, Inc.
c/o Uncle Remus
Regional Library System
1131 East Ave.
Madison, GA 30650

Council of Literary Magazines & Presses
154 Christopher St., Suite 3C
New York, NY 10014-2839

The Dramatists Guild
234 W. 44th St., 11th Floor
New York, NY 10036

Editorial Freelancers Association
36 E. 23rd St., Room 9R
New York, NY 10159

Education Writers Association
1331 H St. NW, Suite 307
Washington, DC 20005
(For those interested in educational writing.)

International Association of Business Communicators
1 Hallidie Plaza, Suite 600
San Francisco, CA 94102

International Association of Crime Writers Inc., North American Branch
JAF Box 1500
New York, NY 10116

International Women's Writing Guild
PO Box 810
Gracie Station
New York, NY 10028
(Open to all women interested in the written word)

Jewish Publication Society
1930 Chestnut St.
Philadelphia, PA 19103
(Promotes Jewish books and culture)

Mystery Writers of America
17 E. 47th St., 6th Floor
New York, NY 10017

National Association of Science Writers
Box 294
Greenlawn, NY 11740

National Writers Club
1450 S. Havana, Suite 424
Aurora, CO 80012
(Association for freelance and would-be freelance writers in all categories)

Appendix B: Writers Organizations

National Writers Union
873 Broadway, Suite 203
New York, NY 10003
(Protects the rights of freelance writers)

PEN American Center
568 Broadway, Suite 401
New York, NY 10012
(Worldwide organization of writers; members support freedom of expression)

Playwrights' Center
2301 Franklin Ave. E.
Minneapolis, MN 55406
(Classes and grants for playwrights)

Poetry Society of America
15 Grammercy Park
New York, NY 10003

Poets & Writers
72 Spring St.
New York, NY 10012

Romance Writers of America
13700 Veterans Memorial Dr., Suite 315
Houston, TX 77014

Science Fiction and Fantasy Writers of America
5 Winding Brook Dr., Suite 1B
Guilderland, NY 12084

Society of Children's Book Writers
22736 Vanowen St., Suite 106
West Hills, CA 91307

Society of Professional Journalists
16 S. Jackson
Greencastle, IN 46135

Society of Southwestern Authors
PO Box 30355
Tucson, AZ 85751
(Help for aspiring and professional writers)

Textbook Authors Association
Box 535
Orange Springs, FL 32182
(Welcomes all authors and prospective authors of textbooks)

Volunteer Lawyers for the Arts
1 E. 53rd St., 6th Floor
New York, NY 10022

Western Writers of America
2800 N. Campbell
El Paso, TX 79902
(For writers dedicated to preserving the spirit of the West)

Women in Communications, Inc.
2101 Wilson Blvd., Suite 417
Arlington, VA 22201

Writers Alliance
PO Box 2014
Setauket, NY 11733
(Support and information for all kinds of writers)

Writers Connection
275 Saratoga Ave. Suite 103
Santa Clara, CA 95050
(Marketing resources and services for writers)

Writers Guild of America (East)
555 W. 57th St.
New York, NY 10019

Writers Guild of America (West)
8955 Beverly Blvd.
West Hollywood, CA 90048

Bibliography

Appelbaum, Judith. *How to Get Happily Published.* New York: Harper & Row, 1988; NAL, 1992.

Aronson, Charles N. *The Writer Publisher.* Arcade, NY: Charles Aronson, 1976.

Boston, Bruce O. (editor). *Stet! Tricks of the Trade for Writers and Editors.* Alexandria, VA: Editorial Experts, 1986.

Bower, Donald and James Lee Young (editors). *Professional Writer's Guide.* Aurora, CO: National Writers Press.

Burgett, Gordon. *The Writer's Guide to Query Letters and Cover Letters.* Rocklin, CA: Prima, 1992.

Burroway, Janet. *Writing Fiction: A Guide to Narrative Craft.* Scott Foresman, 1987.

Carr, Robin. *Practical Tips for Writing Popular Fiction.* Writer's Digest Books.

The Chicago Manual of Style, 14th Edition. Chicago: University of Chicago Press, 1993.

Children's Writer's and Illustrator's Market. Writer's Digest Books. Published annually.

Collier, Oscar, with Frances Spatz Leighton. *How to Write and Sell Your First Nonfiction Book.* New York: St. Martin's, 1994.

Conrad, Barnaby. *The Complete Guide to Writing Fiction.* Writer's Digest Books.

Davidson, Jeffrey P. *Marketing for the Home-Based Business.* Holbrook, MA: Bob Adams, 1991.

Dillard, Annie. *The Writing Life.* Harper, 1989.

Epstein, Connie C. *The Art of Writing for Children: Skills & Techniques of the Craft.* Archon Books, 1991.

Feldman, Elaine. *The Writer's Guide to Self-Promotion and Publicity.* Cincinnati: Writer's Digest Books.

Fry, Ronald W. (editor). *Book Publishing Career Directory.* Hawthorne, NJ: Career Press. Published annually.

Gage, Diane and Marcia Hibsch Coppess. *Get Published: Editors from the Nation's Top Magazines Tell You What They Want.* New York: Henry Holt, 1986.

Giblin, James Cross. *Writing Books for Young People.* The Writer, Inc., 1990.

Goldberg, Natalie. *Writing Down the Bones.* Shambhala, 1986.

Guide to Literary Agents. Writer's Digest Books. Published annually.

Herman, Jeff. *The Insider's Guide to Book Editors, Publishers, and Literary Agents.* Rocklin, CA: Prima Publishing.

Holmes, Marjorie. *Writing Articles from the Heart: How to Write & Sell Your Life Experiences.* Writer's Digest Books.

254 Bibliography

Horowitz, Lois. *Knowing Where to Look: The Ultimate Guide to Research.* Cincinnati: Writer's Digest Books, 1984.

Huddle, David. *The Writing Habit: Essays.* Layton, UT: Gibbs Smith, 1992.

Jacobsohn, Rachel. *The Reading Group Handbook: Everything You Need to Know, from Choosing Members to Leading Discussions.* New York: Hyperion, 1994.

Jerome, Judson. *Poet's Market.* Cincinatti: Writer's Digest Books. Published annually.

Kremer, John. *Book Publishing Resource Guide.* Fairfield, IA: Ad-Lib Publications, 1990.

Literary Market Place. New York: R.R. Bowker. Published annually.

Long, Duncan. *You Can Be an Information Writer.* Port Townsend, WA: Loompanics, 1991.

Macauley, Robie and George Lanning. *Technique in Fiction.* St. Martin's, 1990.

McInerny, Ralph. *Let's Write a Mystery; Let's Write a Novel;* and *Let's Write Short Stories.* Arlington, VA: Vandamere Press/Quodlibetal Features, 1993.

Minot, Stephen. *Three Genres: The Writing of Poetry, Fiction, and Drama.* Prentice Hall, 1988.

National Writer's Union. *The Complete Guide to Freelance Rates and Standard Practice.* Writer's Digest Books.

Neff, Glenda. *The Writer's Essential Desk Reference.* Writer's Digest Books, 1991.

Novel & Short Story Writer's Market. Writer's Digest Books. Published annually.

O'Gara, Elaine. *Travel Writer's Markets: Where to Sell Your Travel Articles and Place Your Press Releases.* Boston: Harvard Common, 1993.

Parinello, Al. *On the Air: How to Get on Radio and TV Talk Shows and What to Do When You Get There.* Hawthorne, NJ: Career Press, 1991.

Pianka, Phyllis Taylor. *How to Write Romances.* Writer's Digest Books.

Polking, Kirk. *Writing Family Histories and Memoirs.* Writer's Digest Books.

Poynter, Dan. *The Self-Publishing Manual.* Santa Barbara, CA: Para Publishing, 1989.

Poynter, Dan and Mindy Bingham. *Is There a Book Inside You? How to Successfully Author a Book Alone or Through a Collaborator.* Santa Barbara, CA: Para Publishing, 1985.

Preston, Elizabeth, Ingrid Monke, and Elizabeth Bickford. *Preparing Your Manuscript.* Boston: The Writer, 1992.

Roberts, Ellen E.M. *The Children's Picture Book: How To Write It, How To Sell It.* Writer's Digest Books, 1984.

Ross, Marilyn and Tom Ross. The Complete Guide to Self Publishing. Cincinnati: Writer's Digest Books.

Ross, Marilyn and Tom Ross. *Marketing Your Books: A Collection of Profit-Making Ideas for Authors and Publishers.* Buena Vista, CO: Communication Creativity, 1990.

Seuling, Barbara. *How to Write a Children's Book and Get It Published.* Charles Scribner's Sons, 1991.

Strunk, William Jr. and E. B. White. *The Elements of Style* (third edition). New York: Macmillan, 1979.

Todd, Alden. *Finding Facts Fast.* Berkeley: Ten Speed Press, 1979.

Tompkins, David G. *Science Fiction Writer's Marketplace and Sourcebook.* Writer's Digest Books.

The Writer's Handbook. Boston: The Writer. Published annually.

Writer's Market. Cincinnati: Writer's Digest Books. Published annually.

Yolen, Jane. *Guide to Writing for Children.* The Writer, 1989.

Zuckerman, Albert. *Writing the Blockbuster Novel.* Cincinnati: Writer's Digest Books, 1993.

Glossary

Abstract. Brief description of chapters for nonfiction book proposal. Also called synopsis.

Adaptation. Rewriting of work for another medium, such as making a novel into a screenplay.

Advance. Money paid to a writer by a publisher before a book is published, against royalty money the book will earn. Advances are usually paid in installments, part at the signing of a contract, part on delivery of a satisfactory manuscript. A good contract will protect an advance if it exceeds royalties earned.

Advance orders. Orders received before a book's publication date.

Advertorial. Advertising in a periodical, formatted to look like editorial material. It will be labeled "Advertising" at the top.

Agent. Acts on behalf of the author to sell manuscripts. Paid a percentage by the author. Agents can present work to appropriate editors and publishers.

All rights. Rights given to a publisher to use a manuscript in any form, anywhere, such as movie or book club sales, without further payment to the author.

Anthology. A collection of works compiled by an editor, on a theme, for example, short fiction by women. The editor secures reprint rights and contracts for unifying writing, such as introductions or commentary.

Auction. Properties an agent believes will be successful may be offered for bidding by publishers. Rights may also be auctioned.

Author tour. Promotional appearances, such as on talk shows and at book stores, by an author, to increase sales of the author's book. Also called book tour.

Author's copies/author's discount. The contract will stipulate the number of free copies, usually 10 hardcovers, an author will receive when the work is printed. The author will receive a discount (40 to 70 percent, depending on quantity) on additional copies to resell at readings.

Authorized biography. A life story written with the permission and cooperation of the subject, or the subject's estate.

Autobiography. A life story written by the person who lived it, often in cooperation with a professional writer.

Backlist. Books still in print by the publisher, but not published in the current season. The backlist may be the mainstay of the publisher's income.

Backmatter. Parts of a book following the main text, including appendices, glossary, bibliography, index and colophon.

Belles lettres. Fine or literary writing.

Bestseller. Titles selling in the largest quantities. Many publications maintain bestseller lists, on a local, regional or national basis.

Binding. The outer part of a book, including the cover, which holds it together. Books now may be hardcover or softcover (paperback). Older books or high-quality specialty books may have leather over the cover.

Biography. An individual's life history.

Bleed. Printing that extended beyond the trimmed edge of a sheet.

Blues/bluelines. Photographic proofs of the printing plates for a book, for final prepress checking and approval.

Blurb. Copy or quotation used to promote a book, as in advertising or on the back cover.

Boilerplate. A standard contract. Usually many changes are made before signing.

Book contract. Legally binding document describing the rights and duties of the author and publisher, setting the terms for advance, rights, royalties, promotion and other contingencies.

Book distribution. Means of getting books from publishers to purchasers. Bookstores are traditional, other ways are direct mail and telemarketing. Publishers may have their own sales staff or make use of independent salespeople or wholesalers.

Book packager. Produces a book from concept to marketing, and sells the package to a publisher or movie producer. Contracts with writers, editors and illustrators. Also book producer, book developer.

Book review. Critical appraisal of a book. A book will be reviewed in trade journals before reviews appear in local and national media. Favorable reviews help book sales, and may be quoted for blurbs.

Books in Print. Annual listing of volumes in print published by R.R. Bowker.

Bound galleys. Uncorrected typesetter's page proofs, bound together and sent to trade journals for review.

Bulk sale. A single purchase of many copies of a title will be discounted.

Byline. The author's name, giving credit for having written a piece.

Camera-ready. Graphic material prepared for a copy camera—black and white, halftones, or line art.

Caption. Describes or explains an illustration or photograph. People in photos are usually identified in the caption. Also called cutline.

Category fiction. See genre fiction.

CD/CD-ROM. Compact discs read by computers, whose contents cannot be modified. Some books are published on CD. See also multimedia, hypertext and interactive fiction.

Chapbook. Small, usually paperback, booklet, of poetry or short fiction.

Clean copy. Manuscript ready for typesetting, without errors, needing no further revision.

Clips. Samples of published work, usually from periodicals.

Coauthor. One of two or more people sharing authorship of a work. Coauthors are given bylines and share royalties based on their contribution.

Collaboration. A writer may collaborate with others who share their expertise. Royalty shares are based on contribution.

Colophon. The publisher's logo; credits for design, composition and production of a book, sometimes describing the typeface, appearing as backmatter or on the copyright page.

Commercial fiction. Fiction written for broad appeal, for widespread sales rather than literary merit.

Concept. The idea around which a book is written.

Contract. Written agreement setting forth the rights and duties of two parties to a sale, such as a publisher and an author.

Contributor's copies. Copies of magazines in which a writer's work appears, sent to the author by the publisher.

Cooperative advertising (co-op). A bookstore advertisement featuring a publisher's book, for which the publisher shares costs.

Glossary

Copublishing. Joint publishing of a book, for example, by a publisher and a museum. An author can sometimes be a copublisher.

Copy. The text of a manuscript.

Copyediting. Editing a manuscript for grammar, spelling, punctuation, clarity and coherence, correctness of facts, and style, including conformity to a publisher's style guidelines.

Copyright. The legal right to reproduce, publish and sell written, musical, and other artistic works. Authors own copyright from the time the work is produced, but to have legal recourse in case of copyright infringement, the work must be registered with the U.S. Copyright Office, and all copies must have a copyright notice. See work-for-hire.

Cover blurbs. Favorable quotations appearing on a book jacket to enhance its sales appeal.

Cover letter. Letter of one page or less that accompanies a manuscript or book proposal, often in response to an editor's request for a manuscript.

Deadline. A due date for submission of work.

Delivery. Submission of completed manuscript to an editor or publisher.

Direct marketing. Advertising directly to a consumer, for example, mailings to selected groups, or order forms in the back of a book.

Display titles. Books produced to be eye-catching at the point of sale.

Distributor. Buys from the publisher to resell at higher cost, to stores, wholesalers, or consumers. Use of distributors can give a publisher greater visibility.

Dot-matrix. Computer printers that produce an image by pushing pins against a ribbon, creating small dots close together. Less than letter-quality. Not to be used for printing a final manuscript.

Dramatic rights. Right to adapt a work for the stage, initially belonging to the author.

Dummy. Mock-up of a book, made by hand.

Dust jacket. Paper wrapper around a hardcover, useful for promotion.

Editor. There are a variety of editorial positions. An executive editor may have chiefly administrative functions; senior and acquisitions editors acquire manuscripts and oversee projects; managing editors have editorial and production duties; associate and assistant editors rewrite manuscripts; copy editors check for style, usage, grammar and punctuation; editorial assistants have clerical and editing duties.

El-hi. Books for elementary to high school reading levels.

Endnotes. In scholarly works, notes appearing at the end of the text, or the end of each chapter, offering explanations or citing source material; as opposed to footnotes, which appear at the foot of the page on which the reference appears.

Epigram. Short, witty phrase, sometimes paradoxical. For example, Oscar Wilde's "I can resist everything except temptation."

Epilogue. In fiction or nonfiction, final segment of text, "after the end," offering commentary or story wrap-up.

Fair use. Provision of copyright law allowing quotation of short passages without infringing on the owner's rights.

Fantasy. A genre featuring magic, wizardry and the supernatural.

Final draft. The last, "polished" version of a manuscript submitted to an editor.

First North American serial rights. Right to publish material in a magazine in the United States or Canada, before it appears in book form.

Flat fee. One-time payment.

Footnotes. Generally found in scholarly works, notes appearing at the bottom of a page, offering further explanation of text or citing a source. Rare in general interest books, in which such information will be integrated into the text or compiled in the biography.

Foreign agents. A foreign entity in a position to buy rights.

Foreign rights. Translation or reprint rights sold in other countries. May be sold as world rights. Often the publisher owns world rights, of which the author may receive a 50 to 85 percent share.

Foreword. Introductory piece written by the author or an expert in the book's field. May be a selling point for a project or finished book.

Frankfurt Book Fair. Every October the world's biggest publishing exhibition, 500 years old, takes place in Frankfurt, Germany.

Frontlist. New titles in a publishing season, receiving priority in a publisher's sales catalog. See backlist.

Front matter. Parts of a book preceding the main text: the frontispiece, title page, copyright page, dedication, epigraph, table of contents, foreword, preface, acknowledgments, introduction, and prologue.

Fulfillment house. A business that fills orders for a publisher, usually for magazines but sometimes for book publishers. Fulfillment houses provide services including warehousing, shipping, and direct marketing response.

Galleys. First typeset version of a manuscript, before division into pages, for proofreading. The last chance to make changes to copy.

Gatefold. A page larger than the book, folded to fit within the book.

Genre fiction. Formula fiction, such as romance, western, science fiction, thriller, horror or mystery. Each genre has subcategories, and falls into a marketing niche. Also called category fiction.

Ghostwriter. Writer who produces material for another under contract, and does not receive credit for the work. For example, an autobiography may be actually written by someone whose name does not appear on the book. Typically paid a flat fee.

Glossary. Alphabetical listing of terms used in a particular field, with definitions.

Glossy. Photographs with a shiny surface, rather than a matte finish.

Graphic novel. Novel published in graphic form, either comic strip or heavily illustrated, of 40 pages or more, in paperback.

Halftone. Photographs are continuous tone, and cannot be reproduced by printing. They are rephotographed by a copy camera with a screen, converting the image to large and small dots for printing.

Hard copy. Printed output from a computer.

Hardcover. Books bound with stiff covers, sometimes wrapped in cloth or leather.

Hi-lo. High interest, low reading level book, appealing to beginning adult readers.

Hook. Concept of a work, catchily expressed.

How-to books. Broad popular category, including instructional works (using software, crafts, home repair), motivational and self-help (psychology, inspiration), and other self-teaching works.

Hypertext. Works which must be presented in computer-readable form, offering search and other linking features. May contain animation, sound and video sequences as well as text. Fiction may have multiple plotlines. See multimedia.

Illustrations. Artwork, photographs or other visual material. Usually purchased separately from a manuscript.

Imprint. A publisher's line or lines of books. Well-known editors may have their own imprint within their publisher's lines.

Instant book. Produced to appear in bookstores as soon as possible after the event it describes; for example, books and CDs about the Gulf War or the O.J. Simpson trial.

Interactive fiction. Works of fiction in print or machine-readable form featuring multiple plots and endings. The reader chooses among alternatives, determining what path the story will take. See multimedia and hypertext.

International copyright. Rights secured for countries observing the International Copyright Convention and respecting the international copyright symbol, ©.

International Copyright Convention. Countries that have signed various copyright treaties. Some treaties require certain conditions to be met at the time of publication.

Introduction. Preliminary remarks preceding text, written by the author or an appropriate authority. If there is a foreword as well, it will not be written by the author. The introduction will be by the author, and more closely tied to the text.

ISBN (International Standard Book Number). Identifying 10-digit number for title and publisher. Used to order and catalog books. Appears on the copyright page, back cover and dust jacket.

ISSN (International Standard Serial Number). Identifying 8-digit number for cataloging and ordering all U.S. and foreign periodicals.

Juveniles. Includes all categories of children's books.

Keyline. Symbols marking position of copy and illustration, in preparation for printing.

Kill fee. Agreed-on portion of contract price received by an author for work on a project subsequently canceled. Not all publishers pay kill fees, such arrangements should be made in advance.

Layout. Arrangement on pages of copy and illustrations; design.

Lead. Opening paragraph which hooks the reader's attention, in a book, periodical article, query letter, proposal or other written material.

Lead title. Frontlist book featured by a publisher in a given season, expected to do well and given the most promotion.

Letterhead. Business stationery imprinted with name, address and logo. An asset for a freelance writer.

Letterpress. High-quality, now outmoded method of printing, currently used for books-as-art. Metal type is inked and pressed directly on the pages.

Letter-quality. Computer printout that looks typewritten, as opposed to dot-matrix printout.

Libel. Defamation of an individual in a published work. Falsehood and malice must be proved, and financial damage incurred, for damages to be awarded to a claimant.

Library of Congress. World's largest library, in Washington, D.C., offering many services. Library of Congress, Central Services Division, Washington D.C. 20540.

Library of Congress Catalog Card Number. Identifying number issued by the Library of Congress to books in its collection. Many libraries use the numbers for their own catalogs.

Literary fiction. Works in which excellent writing has priority over commercial appeal.

Literary Market Place (LMP). Annual directory of the publishing industry, listing publishers and allied businesses, published by R.R. Bowker, available in libraries.

Logo. A symbol identifying a company or product. May be an image, the company's initials or name.

Think of Coca-Cola, IBM, and Apple Computer.

Mainstream fiction. Fiction that is not literary, avant garde or genre, appealing to general readership.

Marketing plan. Selling strategy, including publicity, promotion, sales and advertising.

Mass-market paperback. Lower-cost, smaller-format paperbacks sold from racks in drugstores, supermarkets and other stores. Also called rack editions.

Mechanicals. Typeset copy and art, mounted on boards ready for printing. Also called pasteups.

Middle reader. Books for readers 9 to 11 years old.

Midlist books. Mainstream fiction and nonfiction, expected to be commercially viable but not extremely profitable. Authors should try to present their works as other than midlist.

Modem. Device to connect computers over telephone lines.

Ms, mss. Abbreviation for manuscript(s).

Multimedia. Computer-readable published work, which may include movies, animation, spoken word and music, integrated with text. The user may choose multiple paths through information. If fictional, there may be variable plotlines and outcomes. Presently published mostly on CD, likely to be published on other media and over networks in the future. May be tied-in to print or video publications.

Multiple contract. Book contract including provisional agreement about future book(s).

Net receipts. Amount actually received by a publisher for sales of a book, with returns and discounts subtracted from retail price. Royalties may be based on net receipts rather than the retail price.

Novella. Fictional work falling between a novel and a short story in length.

Offset printing. Most common commercial printing process. Wet ink is transferred from a printing plate to an intermediate surface and then to paper.

One-time rights. Permission to publish a manuscript one time only.

Option clause/right of first refusal. Clause in a book contract stipulating that the publisher has the right to publish the author's next book, but is not obligated to do so.

Outline. Listing of a book's contents, in order, usually in five to 15 double-spaced pages. Used both for proposals and as an aid to writing.

Out-of-print books. Books no longer available from publisher. Usually rights revert to the author.

Over the transom. Submission of unsolicited manuscript by a freelance writer.

Package. The actual, physical book.

Package sale. Manuscript and illustrations bought together.

Page proof. Final typeset copy in page form, before printing.

Paperback. Book bound with a flexible paper cover.

Paperback originals. Usually mass-market fiction published only in paperback, sometimes in hard- and softcover simultaneously. Categories published as paperback originals are increasing.

Parallel submission. Developing several articles on one topic for submission to similar magazines. Different from multiple submission, when the same article may be submitted to several publishers.

Pasteups. See mechanicals.

Payment on acceptance. The editor pays the writer when the manuscript is accepted.

Payment on publication. The writer is paid when the work is published.

Pen name. A name other than one's legal name,

used as a byline when one wishes to remain anonymous. Also called pseudonym.

Permissions. Right to quote or reprint published material, obtained from the copyright holder; for example, a song or poem quoted in a novel requires permission.

Photocopied submissions. A photocopied, rather than original, manuscript submitted to an editor or publisher.

Photostat. Black and white copies reproduced by a photographic process using paper negatives. Only line values are accurate. Also called stat.

Plagiarism. False representation of another's writing as one's own. Illegal with copyrighted work.

Preface. Part of a book's front matter, wherein an author may discuss the genesis of the book, research to produce it, or the philosophy behind it.

Premium. Book sold at reduced price as part of a promotion.

Press agent. See publicist.

Press kit. Promotional package including press release, author biography and photograph, reviews and other information that may pique the interest of a reviewer or those who book author appearances.

Proofreading. Reading a manuscript or galley for typographical errors.

Proposal. Presentation of a book's concept, used to sell the project.

Publication date (pub date). Official date of publication set by the publisher, usually six weeks after books are delivered to a warehouse. Allows time for books to be in stores when promotion begins.

Public domain. Material on which the copyright has expired, or which is uncopyrightable, including government publications, jokes, titles and ideas.

Publicist. Arranges publicity, produces press releases and press kits, books the publicity tour.

Publisher's catalog. Seasonal listing of publisher's new books.

Publisher's discount. Percentage of discount to a retailer, based on quantity purchased.

Publisher's Trade List Annual. Current and backlist catalogs, available in libraries, arranged alphabetically by publisher.

Publisher's Weekly (PW). Main trade journal of the publishing industry.

Quality. In the publishing industry, a book category or format. Quality fiction is presented as fine work, made to high standards.

Query letter. Letter inquiring if an editor is interested in a proposed project, selling both writer and idea.

Reading fee. Sum to read a submitted manuscript, charged by some agents and publishers.

Remainders. Unsold book stock, may be sold very cheaply to bookstores by a publisher and then resold to the public.

Reporting time. Time taken by an editor to report to an author about a manuscript.

Reprint rights. Permission to print an already published work, especially in a different format.

Response time. Time taken by an editor to accept or reject a manuscript and inform the writer of the decision.

Returns. Unsold books returned to a publisher by a bookstore.

Reversion-of-rights clause. In a book contract, a clause stipulating that all rights revert to the author if a book goes out of print or the publisher fails to reprint within a certain time.

Review copy. Free copy of a book sent to reviewer.

Rights. What a writer sells to a publisher.

Rough draft. A manuscript that has not been checked for errors in style, grammar, and punctuation. Usually will be revised and rewritten.

Royalty. A contracted percentage of sales, or net receipts, given to a writer by a publisher.

SASE. Self-addressed stamped envelope. It is customary to enclose an SASE when a reply is expected or desired from an agent or editor.

Satisfactory clause. In a book contract, a clause stating that the publisher may refuse a manuscript not found satisfactory, and require the author to return the advance. Criteria for judging satisfaction should be in the contract, to protect the author.

SCBWI. Society of Children's Book Writers & Illustrators.

Screenplay. Film script, original or adapted from another form.

Second serial rights. Permission to reprint a work in a periodical after its first appearance in a book or magazine.

Self-publishing. The author pays for manufacturing, distribution and marketing of a book, taking all risks and reaping all profits. Successfully self-published works may find subsequent commercial publishers.

Serial rights. Right to publish a manuscript in one or more periodicals.

Series. Books published as a group, based on content or author.

Simultaneous submissions. Submitting the same work to several publishers at the same time. If you are making simultaneous submissions, always mention it in your cover letter. Although it is a common practice, some publishers will not consider such submissions.

Slant. Approach to a topic designed to appeal to readers of a particular publication.

Slush pile. Collection of unsolicited manuscripts submitted to a publisher. Such manuscripts may not be reviewed, and may not be returned without an SASE. Sending a query letter first can help a work avoid the slush pile.

Software. Computer programs.

Solicited manuscript. A manuscript an editor has requested, or agreed to review, before submission.

Speculation. Producing a work without assurance of pay or reimbursement. Also called spec.

Subsidiary rights. All rights beyond first publishing of a book, including reprint, serial, paperback, book club, movie, television, audio- and videotape rights. Rights are specified in a contract.

Subsidy publisher. A publisher who is paid by the author to produce and print a book. More expensive than self-publishing. Also called vanity publisher.

Synopsis. A summary in paragraph, rather than outline, form. Used in proposals to briefly describe a book.

Tearsheet. Page from a periodical containing a writer's work.

Teleplay. Screenplay for television production, accounting for screen dimensions, program length, and placement of commercials.

Terms. Agreed-upon financial conditions in a book contract.

Thumbnail. A tiny rough sketch of a book or magazine layout.

Tip sheet. Element of a press kit, presenting on a single page a book synopsis, marketing data, an author profile and advance blurbs. Also used by sales and publicity departments.

Title page. Page at the front of a book listing title, subtitle, author and other contributors, the publishing house and its logo.

Trade books. Books distributed through traditional channels, bookstores and major book clubs; as opposed to mass-market paperbacks.

Trade list. Catalogs all of a publisher's books in print.

Trade paperbacks. Larger format than mass-market paperbacks, distributed through retail book channels.

Trade publishers. Publish books for general readership, distributed primarily through bookstores.

Transparencies. Color slides.

Treatment. Narrative description of story with sample dialog, in screenwriting.

Unauthorized biography. A life story written without the consent of the subject or the subject's estate or survivors.

University press. Publishing house sponsored by a university, usually nonprofit, publishing mostly books by academics, but also poetry and literary fiction, criticism, and perhaps works of regional interest.

Unsolicited manuscript. Work submitted to an editor or agent without being requested.

Vanity publisher. See subsidy publisher.

Word count. The number of words a manuscript should contain, according to publisher's guidelines. Usually rounded off to nearest 100 words.

Word processor. Computer or software used for writing, editing and storing of text.

Work-for-hire. Commissioned writing, all rights belonging to the publisher or book packager who assigns the work.

Young adult (YA). Books for readers 12 to 18 years old.

Young reader. Books for readers five to eight years old.

Index

A Tale of Two Cities	220
Active voice	54
Adjectives, pairs of	56
Advertising	44
American Online	78, 113
America Online Writers Forum	67
American Federation of Television and Recording Artists (AFTRA)	138, 144-145
American Society of Indexers	72
American Society of Journalists & Authors	165
Antagonist	128, 223
Antithesis	231
Association of Author's Representatives	175
Audio Publishing Association	137
Audiobooks	137-150
Audiofile	143-144
Bar codes	214
Barnes & Noble	104
Blurbs	83-88
Book clubs	17, 96
Book of Virtues, The	109
Book proposals	177
Book reviews	95-108
Book signings	17
Braille Institute	140
Business cards	43, 238
Catalytic event	228
Celestine Prophecy, The	205-206
CD ROM discs	78, 116-117
Characterization	221
Chicago Manual of Style	39, 69
Children's books	183-191

Children's Writer's and Illustrator's Market	188, 190
Cindex	66
Claris Works	207
Classes	17, 23
Classic Books on Cassette	144
Cliches	56
Climax (of a story)	228
Clock (of a story)	224
Community resources	17
Compuserve	78, 113, 114
Concept	129
Conflict	128, 223
Contacts, how to develop	17
Contractions	55
Copyediting	51-62
Copyright	209
Cover letter	155, 190
Coverage	129-135

Desktop publishing	207
Dialog	114
Docutech	211
Dow Jones News Retrieval	115

Fact checking	75-82
Facts (defined)	76
Flap copy	88-92
Freelancing	49, 58, 64, 71

Golden Kite Awards	185
Gone with the Wind	225
Grammar	22

Hamlet	158, 228
Hansel & Gretel	223
Highlights Foundation Writers Conference	187
Homestead Publishing Program	205-217
House style	39

Income chart	8
Indexing	63-73
Information Superhighway	113
Institute of Children's Literature	186
Internet	115-116, 176
Internet Starter Kit	116
Internet Yellow Pages	116
Interviews	118
ISBN number	209-214
Jack and the Beanstalk	222
Knowledge Index	115
Kwik Knowledge	115
Lead	200
Letter writing	18-21
Letterhead	238
Lexis/Nexis	115
Libraries	110-113
Library Journal	97
Library Science Programs	66
Literary Market Place	32, 45, 59, 69, 120
	122, 154, 171, 189
Little Women	223-224
Los Angeles Times Book Review	107
Love interest (fiction)	225
Macbeth	221-223
Macrex	66
Magazines	103, 193-203
Manuscript formats	152
Marketing yourself	15-24
Mechanical editing	52
Medea	222
Microsoft Word	66, 207

Mirror (in fiction)	225
Moonstruck	224
Movie scripts (see Screenplays)	
Narrative hook	220
National Book Critics Circle	166
National Geographic Atlas	77
New book releases	94
New Yorker, The	75
Newsletters	43, 100
NewsNet	114
Newspapers	101, 162
Nexus	78
Nonfiction	231-232
Oxford English Dictionary	77
Pagemaker	66, 207
Passive voice	54
Perfect binding	212
Peter Rabbit	229
Phone calls	21
Plays	126-129
Port Townsend Writer's Conference	187
Premise	227
Prodigy	78
Prologue	221
Proofreading	37-49
Protagonist	128, 221-222
Publisher's reader	25-35
Publishers Weekly	97
Pulp Fiction	230
Punctuation	55
Purple prose	55
Query letter	105-106, 154, 156, 172-174, 190, 197-199

Reader's report	28, 35
Reading critically	219-234
Reading fees	175
Recorded Books, Inc.	143
Research	109-122
Romeo and Juliet	222
Saddle stitching	212
SASE	190
Screenplays	123-126, 128-135
Slush pile	25, 191
Society of Children's Book Writers and Illustrators (SCBWI)	183-186, 191
Solicited manuscripts	25
Spelling	22
Story structure	220
Style	38-39
Subject matter expert	28
Substantive editing	52
Synthesis	231
Tearsheets	69
The Elements of Style	47, 55
The Firm	159, 228
The Prime of Miss Jean Brody	229
Theme	129, 225-227
Thesis	231
Trade journals	202-203
Training	48, 61, 64-65
Truby's Writers Studio	126
Twelve Top Mistakes of Writers	54-57
Under Milkwood	229
Unsolicited manuscripts	25
U.S. Dept. of Agriculture Programs	23, 48, 61-62, 64-65
Video	77

Webster's Dictionary 47
Word Perfect 66, 207
Wordstar 207
Writer's conferences 17, 122
Writers Digest Magazine 104
Writer's groups and organizations 17, 165, 170
Writers guidelines 194
Writers Market 32, 45, 47, 59, 69, 104,
.... 105, 120, 122, 154, 161,
.... 189, 193, 202-203
Writing contests 164-165

Yellow Pages 21, 239

NOTES

NOTES